The Cook Inlet Area

Scale in Miles

0   50   100   200

CartoGraphics by Jon.Hersh, Alaska Northwest Publishing Company

ALASKA

Map Location ➤

Aleutian Islands

Shumagin
Islands

Iliamna

*Iliamna
Lake*

Bristol Bay

ALASKA PENINSULA

Mt. McKinley

ALASKA RANGE

CHUGACH MTS.

Susitna River

Matanuska River

Matanuska Valley

Knik Arm

Knik
(Eklutna)

Knik River

Tyonek

Anchorage

Turnagain Arm

Cook Inlet

Hope

Sunrise
City

*Prince
William
Sound*

Kalgin
Island

Kenai
(Fort Nicholas)

*Sixmile
Creek*

Redoubt Volcano

Tuxedni Bay

Kasilof

Kenai

River

Seward

Iliamna Volcano

KENAI

Chinitna Bay

Ninilchik

Anchor
Point

Homer

PENINSULA

Homer Spit

Iniskin Bay

Augustine Is.

Kachemak Bay

Seldovia

Augustine Volcano

English
Bay

Gulf of Alaska

*Kamishak
Bay*

Point Gore

Cape Elizabeth

Cape
Douglas

Barren
Islands

Afognak Island

Afognak

Kodiak

Pacific Ocean

Kodiak
Island

The Cook Inlet Collection

The Cook Inlet Collection

Two Hundred Years of Selected Alaskan History

Edited by Morgan Sherwood

A collection of curious documents depicting the past economic, social, biological, and geological activity in the Cook Inlet area of Alaska, dating from even before Captain James Cook himself, to just after the Good Friday earthquake, together with brief introductory comments, all comprising a sketchy (at best) history of the state's most populous region.

Illustrations by Diana Tillon

Alaska Northwest Publishing Company
Anchorage, Alaska

Copyright © 1974 by MORGAN SHERWOOD

Printed in U.S.A.

First printing: December 1974
Second printing: March 1975

Library of Congress Catalog Card Number: 74-24638
International Standard Book Number: 0-88240-044-4

Layout and Design: Dianne Hofbeck
Alaska Northwest Publishing Company

For Kristin and Birgit, fellow sourdoughs, who know the answer to a question posed by Frank Fraser Darling in 1969: "You do not need to scratch Alaska bare to get a living now. The greatest wealth of Alaska is still her beauty. . . . How can any of us who love Alaska, who are not just seeking the quick buck, agree indifferently to spoil her fair face?"

Acknowledgments

Special thanks to
The American Council of Learned Societies
The *Anchorage Daily Times*
AP Newsfeatures
Professor Frederica de Laguna, Bryn Mawr College
The Department of Anthropology, Yale University
Human Relations Area Files Press, New Haven
The *International Journal of Environmental Studies*
The Limestone Press, Kingston, Ontario
The *Pacific Northwest Quarterly*
Professor Richard Pierce, Queen's University
The University of Pennsylvania Museum

The Editor

Morgan Sherwood was born and raised in Alaska, and is now professor of history in the University of California at Davis. He wrote *Exploration of Alaska, 1865-1900* (Yale, 1965) and edited *Alaska and Its History* (University of Washington, 1967). He and his wife, Jeanie, divide their time between northern California and Kachemak Bay, in Southcentral Alaska.

Contents

1

Magical Cave Paintings (from Prehistoric Alaska)

by Frederica de Laguna

. . . it seems probable that the cave paintings of Cook Inlet were connected with the religious and magical practices of the prehistoric inhabitants. . . .

Commencing vigorously in the fifteenth century, Europeans began to discover other parts of the world that were never really lost. The explorations were launched in the name of trade, the flag and the cross—mainly the former. By the time Tsarist Russia joined the hunt, a new, more unselfish rationale for exploration had been added: the disinterested search for geographical knowledge.

Russia came tardily but spectacularly into the exploration business. The Kamchatka Expedition, directed by a chubby Dane named Vitus Bering, was a massive attempt to explore eastwardly through Siberia to North America. Bering's second try in 1741, with A. I. Chirikov in command of another vessel, is generally credited with the "discovery" of Alaska by Europeans, though earlier Russian navigators had observed a northern portion of the new continent.

The two captains touched the southern coast of Alaska at several islands. Bering's landfall in the vicinity of Cook Inlet was probably Afognak Island in the Kodiak group, but more than likely Chirikov, on August 1, sighted Cape Elizabeth, the southeasterly gate to Cook Inlet. He noted cryptically in his journal: "At the fifth hour sighted land in N by W, 30 knots; it ended NNW about 18 knots. A walrus dived near the ship. At noon land ended in WNW ½ W, 50 knots; northern ending N by E ½ E, about 30 knots; middle of it NNW ½ W, 20 knots. There were high, snow-covered mountains on the land. During the day flocks of shore ducks and gulls were seen on the wing."

Although the Inlet remained unvisited by the earliest, official Russian explorers, life was not absent from its shores and waters. Two native groups, with complex societies, dwelled in the neighborhood: the Tanaina Athapaskan Indians in the north, and an ancient Eskimo culture whose residence on the southern littoral may have begun before the time of Christ. The Eskimos have been labeled "Kachemak" by Professor Frederica de Laguna, who pioneered the systematic archaeological investigation of these fascinating people. Among other artifacts, they left behind some intriguing art work.

*R*ock paintings at four sites [were discovered] . . . Indian Island, Bear Island and Sadie Cove in Kachemak Bay, and a rock shelter at the head of Tuxedni Bay. The paintings at the first of these sites need not concern us further. They are simply vertical daubs of red paint, about 10 cm. long and from 2 to 3 cm. wide. There are about thirty of these, none more than four feet from the present ground level. The paintings at the other sites are, however, of considerable interest.

The paintings were, I believe, the work of Eskimo, though it is impossible to correlate them with any particular stage of the Kachemak Bay culture. [Cornelius] Osgood reports the Indian tradition that those of Bear Island were made by "people who lived there long ago." The cultural deposits found at three sites—Indian Island, Bear Island, and Tuxedni Bay—point to a considerable antiquity, probably greater than that of any of the known Indian sites in Kachemak Bay. Furthermore, rock paintings are common on Kodiak and Afognak Islands, which the Athabaskans did not reach in their recent migration from the interior, and in Prince William Sound there are rather similar paintings, the Eskimo origin of which is indisputable.

* * *

The paint in every case is red hematite, probably mixed with animal fat. Water, and light applications of gasolene, kerosene, and wood alcohol apparently have no effect on the paint, but wetting with alcohol intensifies the color as long as the surface remains moist. The Tuxedni Bay paintings are a dull brick red; those of Kachemak Bay, especially a few figures at Bear Island, are brighter. The pigment at the last mentioned site is far from uniform, which suggests that the paintings were made over an interval of time. The surface of rock was never prepared. The paintings at Tuxedni Bay may have been made with the finger, as one of Osgood's informants suggests, or with the frayed end of a stick. Those at Sadie Cove and Bear Island were certainly painted with a finer instrument.

The paintings at Tuxedni Bay are arranged in eight main groups, as determined by the joint planes of the rock. No real attempt at composition is evident, however, and the members of a group are not even drawn to the same scale. The figures are not always vertical. . . .

An identification of the subjects represented is difficult. The most prominent figure, which dominates the whole group, and can even be seen from the water's edge, suggests the conventionalized symbol used by the Eskimo of Bering Strait to represent the raven. For the Indians of the Northwest Coast, including the Eyak of the Copper River delta and the Athabaskans of Cook Inlet, all of whom possess the dual social organization of eagle (or wolf) and raven moieties, such a symbol would undoubtedly be of totemic significance. But for the prehistoric Eskimo of Cook Inlet we should have to offer another explanation, since it is unlikely that they had this type of social organization. . . .

There are seven representations of men (or perhaps of bears or anthropomorphic figures). On four the penis is indicated; on two it is clearly lacking. On the seventh, we cannot be sure if it is the penis or a tail. Other characteristic features are the broad, somewhat flattened head, suggesting an animal's muzzle, the widespread arms and legs, and the round, squat bodies. . . . While these pictures seem to be men, we must not overlook the possibility that they may represent bears, or even human beings disguised as bears. In view of the unique position which the bear occupies in the religious concepts of both northern Indians and Eskimo, we might well expect that in art, too, the bear might have more of the human than the animal.

Four figures seem to represent men in kayaks. In recent years two- or three-man bidarkas were more common on Cook Inlet and neighboring waters than the kayak for a single person. Unfortunately the pictures are too crude to give us much idea of the shape of the kayak. The stern was apparently rather short and the bow considerably upturned. The shape of the prow reminds us a little of the kayaks of the Canadian Thule culture. The kayaks of Cape Espenberg in Kotzebue Sound, and of King and Nunivak Islands, Alaska, also have an upturned prow, but those of the last two localities are pierced by a hole. The modern bidarkas of the southwestern Alaskan Eskimo have divided prows. The paintings may, therefore, furnish archaeological proof that the ornamented prows of the modern Alaskan kayaks are a recent feature, and that the original kayak was like that of the Canadian Thule culture.

One of the kayakers is apparently wearing a hunting hat or helmet with a brim, like those worn until recent times by the southern Eskimo and the Aleut.

Two objects seem to be umiaks. The first and last upright elements may be the bow and stern of the boat, but they are more probably the occupants. Thus, one boat carries six, the other seven persons. Analogous representations of men in boats are familiar from archaeological sites in Europe and Siberia. . . .

Other figures represent whales. One of these can be identified as a killer whale. Two, however, are indistinct and may possibly be quadrupeds of some sort. There is also a swan (?), the eye of which is formed by a naturally dark spot on the rock. . . .

The paintings at Bear Island are much finer and smaller in scale than those of Tuxedni Bay; the reproductions are natural size while the Tuxedni Bay pictures have been reduced to one-third. The surface of the rock is considerably broken up, and the pictures are scattered with little reference to each other.

There are two human figures. The man suggests by his flattened head the human figures of Tuxedni Bay, though the elongated proportions of the body are different. We should also note the fingers on the left hand. The second figure is that of a pregnant woman; the head is cut off by a break in the rock. This picture is very different from anything else found in this region. Perhaps the closest parallel would have to be sought in the European Paleolithic. There are two other anthropomorphic (?) figures.

Several pictures are probably seals, sea otter, or similar sea mammals. Four appear to be wounded with harpoons or darts. The knob at the end of the shaft sticking into the side of one of these is

5

evidently the bladder attached to the dart or harpoon used with the throwing board.

The other animals are difficult to identify. There are two quadrupeds standing on their hind legs (?), the third figure in the same group is a shark (?). There is a kid or faun, a bear (?), a walrus (?), a whale, and a fox or other quadruped. The cross-like figure is suggestive of a conventionalized living form, perhaps that of a flying bird. . . .

The paintings at Sadie Cove are the most interesting from an artistic point of view, for they offer the only example of true composition. They are larger than those of Bear Island. Their size and the motif of the leaping whale point towards Tuxedni Bay. Only one group of paintings was found. The paint has weathered badly, the upper left-hand portion being completely obliterated. There were doubtless four whales originally, and the upper band, composed like the lower of highly conventionalized land animals, formerly extended across the whole group. The whales are blackfish, very well drawn, and in characteristic action. The land animals, however, cannot be identified.

That these paintings were not intended primarily as works of art is evident from the fact that they are all more or less remote from the permanent villages, and that no paintings were found on convenient rock surfaces near village sites. The modern Indians and Eskimo about Kachemak Bay whom I questioned know nothing definite about the pictures. Anisim, the Kodiak Eskimo living near Seldovia, said that on Kodiak Island there were many such paintings and that they were "like letters," to tell others of game which had been killed. . . . A woman from Afognak, an island in the Kodiak group, said that formerly only the "old people" (the initiated?) made these paintings, and that they were to bring good luck in hunting. Alec Mishikof, a Kenai Indian, the nephew of a shaman, was inclined to connect the paintings with the whale killers. He was the best informed on magical and religious matters of any of the natives that I met, though he insisted that the Kenai Indians also had a secret society of whale killers, like the Eskimo. This statement was vigorously denied by the other Indians at Kenai. The figures of whales which appear at the three sites certainly support his belief that they were made by whalers. The harpooned seals of Bear Island also suggest a hunting ritual. Alec Mishikof thought that the rock shelters were the secret places where the whalers used to boil out the human fat from which they made poison for their lance blades. Afterwards, the bones had to be reassembled (with pitch, he hazarded) and fed regularly, otherwise the skeleton would pursue the whaler and devour him. Our excavations at Tuxedni Bay, Bear and Indian Islands, however, did not uncover any human remains.

* * *

While we dare not hazard a definite explanation, it seems probable that the cave paintings of Cook Inlet were connected with the religious and magical practices of the prehistoric inhabitants, that the knowledge of their location and perhaps of their meaning was secret, and that they were directed to secure good luck in hunting or in other activities. Under the circumstances and by whom they were made—by adolescents, by whalers or some other shamanistic society—must remain a mystery unless ethnological investigations on Kodiak Island be not too late to find the solution. ▓

2

Tanaina Tales

by Cornelius Osgood

*. . . [natives] at Iliamna, Tyonek, and Kenai said that . . .
[seagulls] were eaten, and insisted they are good. De
gustibus non est disputandum.*

Unlike the Eskimo, the Tanaina do not sing while fighting.

*A hunter should not kill a bird or animal which has
claws if he is with a pregnant woman.*

Both the Eskimos and the Tanainas relied on the Inlet's
abundant and varied natural resources. Some of their
food-gathering technologies were ingenious, and their appetites were
catholic. In addition to sharing the region's rich wildlife, they also
shared warlike habits. Their oral history is complete with war stories
of the kind that decorate the literary history of the "civilized" western
nations. Both native cultures had their own superstitions, to which in
modern society we give the names theology and science.

*T*he ordinary native method of catching salmon is to construct a weir by damming a creek or small river with a construction of logs and debris set diagonally upstream from each side toward a small opening in the center through which the fish are forced to pass, thus entering a V-shaped trap of logs about ten feet on a side, from which they cannot extricate themselves. One man stands in the trap and with a small dip-net takes out two or three fish at a time, which another man kills with a club. A third man puts a spruce root line through their gills (or throws them into a boat) and brings them ashore. Sometimes, instead of the simple fish weir, the Indians make a basket trap of long alders with a conical entrance which they place at the opening of the dam. They remove the fish from a door in the same manner as described above. The Kachemak Bay Tanaina do not use a gaff-hook in fishing, but at Kenai the latter instrument serves for catching crabs.

The Tanaina also catch fish by the use of a drag-net made of alder poles tied together with spruce root line. Men take hold of each end, and with another man in the middle, they push the fish into shallow water, where they kill them with wooden clubs. Sometimes the fish are pushed on to flats where they strand at low tide. When all the fish have been taken ashore, an old man counts and divides them equally. The women clean the fish, the boys wash them, and old men hang them up to dry.

The Tanaina also employ fish spears to catch salmon, but it is a much slower method requiring a good eye and considerable dexterity.

Herring are common over the whole inlet during the spring and summer, but the natives do not eat many. They complain that they have too many bones.

Halibut are every place in the Kachemak Bay area during the summer, retiring to deep water in the winter. There are few around Tyonek in the summer and Kenai people declare they do not fish for halibut. For other parts of the Tanaina area, these fish are not available. Halibut the Kachemak Bay natives catch in the following fashion. At low tide they drive a stick into the beach so that it stands about three feet high. At the top of this stick they tie another about a foot long. Then, taking a spruce root line, with the bark on, and about as thick as a finger, they fasten it at one end to a rock, heavy for two men to lift. This they place on the tidal beach at the base of the upright stick. Next they tie the line at the base of the upright stick, then at the top, and finally at the end of the smaller stick, the remainder of the line dropping so as to suspend a large fishhook about one foot above the beach. The fishermen bait the hook with a humpback salmon about fourteen to sixteen inches long. The hook, after the salmon is split open, is inserted so that the barb comes a little way out of the back. Small halibut cannot take this hook and bait, but when the tide is in, a big halibut is often attracted. In taking the bait, the halibut breaks the small stick and perhaps the large one, but the great fish is held by the heavy rock. By taking advantage of the tide, the fishermen cleverly avoid a breaking weight on the line, for as the tide goes out, the people have great enjoyment in seeing the halibut left stranded on the beach.

* * *

The animals of the woods and mountains, besides fish, are of great importance to the Tanaina food-hunters. Fortunately they are plentiful, and with the exception of the brown bear, the mountain sheep and goat, range in easy reach of the hunters of every village.

Ordinarily several men go on a hunting trip together; only if a man is to be gone for a considerable length of time does he take his wife along. Generally the party includes an old man who will stay in the camp and help to get the food ready. At night he tells stories. A hunter carries a spear, bow and arrows, and a knife, besides a blanket and a bag containing implements for making a fire. Also some dried fish and seal oil may be taken along to eat in case nothing is killed. The spear is seven or eight feet long if it is to be used in mountains, or three or four feet if in bush country where there is little room for manipulation. The hunter carries it in the right hand and the bow in the left. Having approached sufficiently close to the animals which he wants to kill, he drops the spear, reaches his right hand above his right shoulder to the quiver, from which he draws an arrow, putting it to the bow with only the simple movement of raising and lowering the arm. The arrow is shot toward the heart. When the time for shooting has past, the hunter drops his bow and takes his spear in both hands for the ending of the struggle.

The Kachemak Bay Tanaina always take off their footwear to run down game. This means severe bruising of the feet from the thorny devil-weeds. Nevertheless, they consider it necessary in order to outrun the animal pursued, which is all the hunter thinks about. . . .

* * *

The Tanaina country benefits from a good supply of game birds, part of which, however, is limited by the seasons. Ducks of many varieties begin to arrive, according to the Indians, from March to April and do not leave for the winter until October. The natives generally catch them with snares, but sometimes they use the sling-shot successfully.

Geese are available about the same times as the ducks. The Tanaina snare them and occasionally shoot them by means of the bow and arrow.

Swans are considered tough by some and good by others. In the Upper Inlet they arrive with the ducks and geese to lay their eggs in the small lakes and stay all summer.

Loons are reported as seasonal except in Kachemak Bay which enjoys the mildest climate. There, loons remain in the winter. The natives shoot the loons from boats if they can approach closely enough to prevent them from flying. The bird is slow to lift itself from the water and consequently fears to make the attempt in

13

danger, preferring rather to escape by diving. Loons are very much liked by some people although they are notoriously tough.

Sea gulls, like the loons, remain in the lower part of the inlet during the winter. My principal Kachemak Bay informant said they are not eaten but are killed for bait. In the Upper Inlet it is said only the eggs are eaten. On the other hand, informants at Iliamna, Tyonek, and Kenai said that they are eaten, and insisted they are good. *De gustibus non est disputandum.*

Ptarmigan too are seasonal, as far as hunting is concerned, for in summer they retire to the mountains, practically out of reach. In the winter, when they come to the flats, however, the people snare them or sometimes they merely hit them with stones.

Grouse, like ptarmigan, are fine eating and easy to kill. They also are more often hunted in winter. Like the porcupine, they often save the weary traveler from his hunger. The Indians sometimes kill them in deadfalls, more occasionally with sticks. A rock thrown over the head of the bird frightens it into thinking a hawk is attacking. The hunter can then approach closely to kill it.

Eagles and owls, of which there are several varieties, all the Tanaina eat, except perhaps the small night owl. These latter are shot by boys, sent out by old men at night who do not like their cries. The owls are then thrown away. Besides shooting with arrows from an ambush in a clump of trees, the natives catch eagles and owls in snares. The feathers, particularly of the eagle, are desired. . . .

The raising of birds is not unknown. A Kachemak Bay informant told how young eider ducks are enticed to the hand by honking like the mother bird. They are then kept like chickens in a little house. As they grow up they sometimes wander as far as a mile from home, but always return to the same house. Their wings are not clipped. When the birds are grown they are eaten. This information was verified at Kenai. At Iliamna it is said that young geese and sea gulls, as well as ducks, are kept as pets. The informant insisted, however, that such birds are never eaten, they are just friends, with which to play.

Extremely common are many kinds of berries which are gathered by the women during the months of July (especially around Kachemak Bay) and August. The natives find red salmon berries everywhere but white ones only in the Kachemak Bay region. The red and black currants and the blueberries are unusually large, and the red raspberries as sweet as sugar. Both high- and low-bush cranberries are plentiful as well as blackberries.

Spruce fiber, and sometimes birch, taken from under the bark in May (it tastes of pitch in June and July) the Tanaina consider good. Also brown spruce gum is chewed.

Willow buds are not eaten. The Indians in the Kenai and Upper Inlet areas gather wild rice. Also at Kenai there are "wild peas," some kind of seeds in a pod, found on the seashore in August. Wild onions are said to be eaten by the Tyonek and the Kachemak Bay people.

Fern roots are dug, according to Kenai informants, and their location is remembered so that they may even be found under the snow. One variety of root, eaten at Tyonek, may have been the same. But by far the most important root is the klila, which grows only in the Upper Inlet. This parsnip-like root is the principal trade article of the district and is transported from one end of the region to the other. The Upper Inlet people dig the root in the flats along the shore with the aid of a short stick during the month of September.

Around Kachemak Bay, two types of edible seaweed are collected any place off shore. The seaweeds are not available elsewhere in the inlet, however.

Upper Inlet natives boil wild rosebuds to make a drink like tea. Mushrooms are not eaten.

None of these vegetable foods the Tanaina attempt to cultivate, but many, particularly berries, they store for winter use.

* * *

The leadership of a Tanaina war party on the offensive is apparently in the hands of the toyon, or head chief, and constitutes one of the few occasions on which he leaves his village. The fighters are always young men which perhaps explains why the toyon as an older person is always described as giving orders from the rear. The true battle leader is the second chief, who leads his men to attack, half dancing as they agilely dodge the arrows and spears of their enemy. Unlike the Eskimo, the Tanaina do not sing while fighting. If successful in the conflict, they kill all the enemy warriors except two or three whom they release, and take prisoner all the women and children. An Upper Inlet Indian gave the only dissenting evidence, saying the women and children are also killed. The same informant clearly corroborates the revenge motive for war. He gloats over the visualization of the survivors of a massacred party telling the tragedy to the relatives of the dead.

The bodies of those on both sides killed in war are commonly burned and the bones buried. Likewise the possessions of the victims are said always to be burned or destroyed. . . . The joints of victims are not cut, but the Iliamna warriors admit to cutting off the heads of male victims and hanging them up. Also among the same people the ashes of the dead enemy are used by shamans as a poison for anointing hunting knives. This latter statement is similar to that given by Eskimo informants at English Bay on the lower east coast of Cook Inlet who describe poison made from the fat of dead people and used for poisoning whale spears. Head hanging and poison making as described at Iliamna are either unknown or denied by informants elsewhere, however. . . .

As an ending to this section on warfare, a brief story may be interesting.

A group of Tanaina living on an island in Kuska Bay (lower Cook Inlet) were attacked by a party of Eskimo from Kodiak. The island occupied by the beseiged had one side which was steep while the other sloped off into a beach. The exposed area was protected, however, by a palisade built of upright poles which were lashed together by means of skin lines. The fortifications proved sufficient to withstand the attacks of the besiegers and the Indians held out easily until they were weakened by the lack of drinking water of which they had no natural supply on the island. Finally one man took two seal stomachs and swam ashore under water. He came to the surface where a small stream fell precipitously into the sea. After filling the bags, he tied them to his waist and swam back to the island, where under the cover of darkness both he and his cargo were hauled up to safety. Not satisfied with this exploit, the hero swam under water to the Eskimo kaiaks whose occupants were maneuvering them for an attack on the island. With his knife he ripped open the seal skin cover of one from the bottom and it rapidly sank. The unexpectedness of this action precipitated so much confusion on the part of the Eskimo that several more boats were sunk in the same way. The occupants attempted to save themselves by getting into other kaiaks but these sank from over-loading and finally the whole party had to swim for shore. As they landed, attempting to shield themselves against the precipitous side of the island, the Indian women hit them on the head with rocks.

This story was given by a Kachemak Bay informant as a true account of a battle but it is remembered by him more obviously for the pleasure of recreating a picture of Indian women hitting Eskimos on the head with rocks.

* * *

The following superstitions were collected from various informants in the several villages as they chanced to come out in conversations. They undoubtedly represent only a small fraction of the number which are current among the Tanaina.

Animals may not be brought into a house through the door, but must be lowered through a hole in the right rear corner of the barabara. Young boys or girls are not allowed to walk by that corner. (Caribou, sheep and moose are exceptions to the rule; after hanging outside one night they may be brought in through the door.)

Dogs are not allowed to chew bones of any animals except moose or caribou. Trout bones are also taboo to dogs.

Feathers are put through the nostrils of ducks when caught.

Men may not kill dogs—it would spoil their luck at hunting (they let the old women do it).

The eating of very fresh meat or fish is said to make people (especially women) very nervous and even die. By first taking a sweat bath the evil effects can be avoided.

It is bad luck for young people to eat fish when it is very greasy.

A menstruating woman never walks on the beach.

For young people to step on blood would make them crazy.

To kill a brown ermine in winter is a bad omen.

If a black bear, when dying, falls on its back with its paws out and moans, it means that a friend will die.

It is a bad omen when an animal being killed does not die immediately. (Once when my principal Kachemak Bay informant was young, he proceeded to kill a seal by smashing its head but when he got it home, it was still alive. That night when he skinned it, it still quivered. A month afterwards his father died.)

If a young man has a few white hairs over his ears, it is said that he will live to be a very old man. Yellow hairs in the same place indicate an early death.

A whistling sound in the fire is said to be a good omen. (This does not refer to the peculiar noise made by a spirit which the Indians reward by throwing in food.)

If a mouse and a frog fight together, it is a bad omen.

If a frog comes into a house, it is a bad omen. (It is best for the occupants to leave the house.)

If a little owl flies counter-clockwise and sits on the roof of a house, and does this performance three times, the owner will die within half a year.

If small animals brought home as pets run counter-clockwise, blood will run from their mouths and they will die.

A hunter should not kill a bird or animal which has claws if he is with a pregnant woman.

A necklace of claws is fastened around a baby's neck to make him strong. (He will then later kill any animal he sees.)

White wood worms tied around each wrist of a baby boy make him strong.

It is bad luck if someone gains possession of a man's potlatch drum.

A buzz-toy (apparently a kind of bull-roarer) is swung on the beach when the waves are rolling in in order to make fine weather.

Offerings of food are said to be made to rocks on top of the pass between Kamishak Bay and Iliamna Lake.

3

A Lost European Colony in 16th Century Alaska?

by Richard Pierce

. . . [He] inferred that the old Russian settlement . . . supposedly founded by Novgorodians fleeing from their birthplace about 1571 . . . was discovered on Kenai Peninsula. . . .

Along with the Tanaina Indians and Kachemak Eskimos, a third culture may have been at home on Cook Inlet one hundred years before Captain Chirikov sailed by, or so American and Soviet scholars have speculated until recently. The issue was settled in a new book by Dr. Svetlana G. Fedorova of the Institute of Ethnography in the U.S.S.R. Academy of Sciences. An American writer, from sketchy information, had "inferred that the old Russian settlement . . . supposedly founded by Novgorodians fleeing from their birthplace about 1571 . . . was discovered on Kenai Peninsula . . .," near Kasilof, according to Fedorova. Richard Pierce catalogs the events leading to this dramatic (and improbable) "discovery."

19

*T*he following item from the *Anchorage Daily Times,*
30, June 1937, sent . . . [to me] recently by a correspondent
in Alaska, reveals the genesis of the much discussed "Russian"
village.

The possibility that Eskimo tribes penetrated southward in
Alaska as far as the Kenai Peninsula was seen in the discovery of
a partially buried village by a member of a Public Survey Office
field party which recently completed surveying 30,000 acres
there for homesteading purposes.

Floyd G. Betts, U. S. cadastral engineer and L. M. Berlin, land
surveyor are now in Anchorage with other members of the
survey party after spending April, May, and most of June in the
Kenai section. They plan to leave soon for Alaska Railroad points
to continue survey work.

This discovery of the village was made by P. O. Lucha,
University of Alaska student who was a member of the Otto
William Geist St. Lawrence Island Eskimo expedition in 1934-35.

The village was completely covered by overburden, estimated
by Mr. Lucha to be at least 300 years old. Belief that Eskimos
may have established the village was upheld by the striking
similarity in structure and design to other villages known to be
Eskimo, Mr. Lucha said.

Tree date lines showed the village to be at least 300 years old.
There were 31 well preserved houses, a partial excavation
showed. Each house was approximately 15 feet by 22 feet in size,

and stood about 14 feet in height. The cabin walls are approximately four inches thick, made of beach sand bricks, logs and sod. Each house has a fireplace in the center made of rocks of volcanic origin. . . .

While the villages have been discovered from time to time along the waterways, the unusual feature of this lost city, Mr. Lucha pointed out, lies in the fact that it is situated miles from any water supply. This fact, according to Mr. Lucha, is indicative of great change in the terrain—that water must at one time have been in the nearby area, and has since shifted. . . .

The newspaper account would of course be less accurate than engineer Floyd G. Betts' report, summarized by Dr. Fedorova. The journalist mentions bricks and logs, not found in Betts' account. Neither, however, ascribes the village to Russians.

Similar phrases indicate that the news story was almost certainly the basis for the eleven line summary in Merle Colby's *A guide to Alaska* . . . [1939]. Colby adds that the village was "many miles from the coastline," but he, too, says nothing about a Russian connection unless one implies that from mention on the same page of the Russian settlement of St. Nicholas, and that of St. George, at Kenai. The *Guide* was a collection of facts from secondary or tertiary sources, and of regional lore, written in a popular vein. One of the Federal Writers Project guidebooks, it received the routine sponsorship given each book in the series by the governor of the state or territory concerned, in this case by Governor John W. Troy.

This brief reference caught the eye of Theodore S. Farrelly (1883-1955), a writer who for years had interest in the early colonization of Alaska by the Russians. As early as 1931 he wrote "A Reported Sixteenth Century Settlement in Alaska," *Journal of American History* [1931]. . . . It is unlikely that Farrelly knew Russian, and what he cites vaguely as documents from the Valaam Monastery are, as Dr. Fedorova indicates, probably a translation of the published letters of the monk German regarding the alleged refugees from Novgorod in the time of Ivan the Terrible who somehow crossed Siberia before it was even conquered and settled in Alaska.

For Farrelly, the brief reference to the Kenai find in the Colby volume made it all fit together. Combining this with the monk German's story he deduced that the settlement was Russian, stating that "Details of the discovery are given in a recent report published under the auspices of John W. Troy, the Governor of Alaska." That is, Colby's *Guide* as mentioned above. Governor Troy's actual report for 1937 does not even mention the discovery.

Farrelly's article was noted in the U.S.S.R. by Academician A. V. Efimov . . . (1948). Efimov quotes "the American historian Farrelly" and his conclusions, based on "a report by John W. Troy, the Governor of Alaska," and seems to view the Russian connection as a fact. Taking Efimov's lead, other Soviet scholars have repeated the story, and have speculated on it at length giving it a dignity out of all proportion to the dubious original. This "evidence"—a newspaper report of an undoubtedly hasty examination of a village site by a surveying party, reviewed briefly in a popular guidebook, from which an enthusiastic amateur made unfounded deductions, accepted uncritically by scholars handicapped by distance and by a constricted flow of information has caused a great waste of time. Working from other evidence Dr. Fedorova rightly concludes that the story is baseless. In the absence of anything linking the Kasilof site to Russians, the whole thing should be thrown out once and for all as irrelevant to the problem of early Russian settlement in Alaska. The lessons that should be drawn are the need for prompt examination, by competent personnel, of newly discovered historic or prehistoric sites in Alaska—which has in fact been improving in recent years—and closer contact between Soviet and North American scholars, permitting freer exchange of information and more accurate evaluation of sources.

4

An Ecological Mystery

by H. J. Lutz

. . . caribou on the Kenai Peninsula "vanished as rapidly as the buffalo when modern rifles were sold to the natives by enterprising American traders."

The question of whether a long-lost European colony dwelled on Cook Inlet was resolved easily, if tardily. The whereabouts over time of two important species of wildlife was more difficult to determine. The celebrated Kenai moose may not have ranged along the eastern shores of the Inlet when Chirikov sighted Cape Elizabeth, but the Peninsula may have been the home of caribou that no longer roam the area. Over the years, naturalists have worried about the appearance and disappearance of these magnificent animals. Did forest fires spoil the caribou's graze and prepare the way for vegetation more delectable to the moose? Did Daniel Elliott's "head hunters, both white and red," exterminate the moose earlier, and the caribou recently? Or does some other natural agent explain the environmental mystery surrounding the moose and caribou of Kenai Peninsula? H. J. Lutz, a professor of silviculture, discusses part of the evidence in his study of the ecological effects of forest fires.

*T*he preponderance of evidence favors the conclusion that moose are today common or abundant in some regions throughout the North where formerly they were rare or not known to exist. This has been repeatedly asserted with regard to the Kenai Peninsula, a region now famous for both the numbers and size of its moose. In 1901 [Wilfred] Osgood stated, "According to report the moose has but recently appeared in the Cook Inlet region; the older Indians say no moose were there when they were boys." Similar statements were made by others. . . . [Frank] Dufresne described the situation as follows:

> In the year 1883 a forest fire raged for months on Kenai Peninsula. Shortly thereafter the caribou herds vanished. Coincident with this rapid passing of the caribou appeared the moose which were practically unknown on the Kenai before the big fire. Today, not a single caribou exists on the Peninsula, but the place is famous for its moose herds. The explanation is not complex. Fire destroyed the lichens on which the caribou feed; fire produced in its wake abundant growths of willow, birches, and cottonwoods relished by the moose.

That moose were practically unknown on the Kenai Peninsula before the fire of 1883, mentioned by Dufresne, may be doubted. In the Tenth Census of the United States, 1880, [Ivan] Petroff described certain delicacies served at a native feast . . . (on the north side of the Kenai River, above the village of Kenai) and specifically mentioned dried moose nose. In addition, he stated, "The variety of native animals is very great. . . . The deer here is apparently a larger cousin of the reindeer, the woodland caribou. Moose, single and in family groups, can be found feeding through the low brushwood and alder swamps." [W. R.] Abercrombie, in his report of 1884, quoted Ivan Petroff, who was then in the Customs Service at Kodiak, as follows: "Forage can be gathered in the vicinity of Fort Kenai during the summer to keep the stock during the winter. The climate is not more rigid than that of Montana. Moose abound, furnishing an article of food preferable to beef." Petroff was familiar with the Cook Inlet region and must have written the above statement not more than a year or two after the fire of 1883. . . .

The Eleventh Census of the United States, 1890, only 7 years after the fire of 1883, contains a statement on the Kenai Peninsula, as follows: "The forests and valleys of this region are still filled with numerous droves of moose . . . and furnish a rich hunting ground for the Tanainas of Nikishka and Kenai." That moose were actually present on the Kenai Peninsula at a very early date is demonstrated by the findings of [Frederica de] Laguna in her excavations on Yukon Island in Kachemak Bay on the south end of the peninsula. Moose bones were found in four layers representing four periods of habitation.

Fires, through their effect on vegetation, probably favor an increase in the population of moose, but there is no proof that burning was uncommon on the peninsula prior to 1883. Apparently the earliest written record of a forest fire in Alaska is that of the Russian mining engineer [Petr Doroshin]. . . .

The available history of moose on the Kenai Peninsula was investigated because the presence or absence of fires does not satisfactorily explain the appearance and disappearance, or the existence of large or sparse populations of these animals. In this connection it may be pointed out that in the discussion of the paper by [Edward] Chatelain, Urban C. Nelson remarked, "I think probably the conclusion that the moose abundance there [on the Kenai Peninsula] is purely the result of burns might be open to question."

* * *

In the treatise on the deer family by [Theodore] Roosevelt and others, Andrew J. Stone prepared the section on moose. He offered an interesting explanation for the increase in the moose population in various areas, including the Kenai Peninsula, as follows:

> They are now numerous in a very large territory in northwest British Columbia, through the Cassiar Mountains, on Level Mountain, and throughout the head waters of the Stickine River, where thirty years ago they were unknown. They are now abundant on the Kenai Peninsula, Alaska, and in other sections of the North where at one time they did not exist. Acquisition of territory by so wary an animal as the moose can only be accounted for in one way. Many years ago the Indian tribes occupying these sections were very numerous and inimical to moose life, but, since the Indians have dwindled from thousands to insignificant numbers, the moose finds comparatively unmolested life. This I know to be the case on the Kenai and in the country referred to in northwest British Columbia; and there are many similar changes in conditions in other parts of the North, notably in the Nahanna River country, north of the Liard, where the entire tribe of Indians that once hunted the country have died out, to the very great increase of moose.

* * *

The problem of fires and caribou is in a category wholly different from that of fires and moose. Unlike the moose, which prefers pioneer plant communities or at least vegetation representing early stages of successional development, the barren ground caribou normally lives in environments characterized by climax plant communities, tundra, and forest-tundra transition.

Movements of caribou exhibit some of the same vagaries noted in the movements of moose. In early times, for example, caribou were known on the Kenai Peninsula, but are not now present. Perhaps the last caribou observed in the region is that mentioned in 1912 by [George] Shiras who wrote "a good-sized stag was seen south of Benjamin Creek by a party of surveyors last July [1911?]." Dufresne associated the disappearance of caribou from the Kenai country with a forest fire that burned in the region in 1883. Other reasons for their vanishing have been suggested by earlier writers.

Daniel G. Elliot observed, "On the Kenai Peninsula and surrounding districts head hunters, both white and red, have nearly exterminated the species, and the increased means of transportation to and through their country, the large number of hunters, greatly added to annually, and the improved firearms, would seem to foretell the extinction in a brief period of this fine animal in the regions where he is accessible."

[J. A.] Allen, writing of the specimen of caribou that Andrew J. Stone collected on September 24, 1900, quoted Stone as follows: "Caribou . . . are already very scarce on the Kenai Peninsula, and will doubtless soon be exterminated, the region being greatly frequented by visiting sportsmen, while native hunters kill the moose and caribou for their heads, disposing of them at good prices for shipment to San Francisco." And [John C.] Phillips remarked that the caribou on the Kenai Peninsula "vanished as rapidly as the buffalo when modern rifles were sold to the natives by enterprising American traders." As late as 1898 large bags of caribou were at least occasionally taken. Thomas C. Dunn, President of the Munina Alaska Gold Mining Co., in an account of a hunting expedition in 1898 of Harry C. Lee, stated that Lee found game abundant between the . . . upper end of Kachemak Bay and Tustumena Lake. Lee killed three caribou.

It seems reasonably certain that the increased tempo of burning by forest fires in Alaska since 1890 unfavorably affected caribou populations. Extensive forest fires, particularly in the lichen-rich forest-tundra transition or woodland areas, have without doubt destroyed large portions of the caribou range. Unlike moose browse, which in favorable circumstances may develop in a few years following fires, caribou range requires very many years for recovery after it has been damaged by fire or by overgrazing.

5

A Northwest Passage? Not Likely (1778)

by James Cook

*I was now fully persuaded that I should find no passage
by this inlet; and my persevering in the search of it
here, was more to satisfy other people, than to confirm
my own opinion.*

*C*aptain Cook was the first European explorer in the Inlet. When
he came upon Cape Elizabeth (which he named) in May 1778, he
had behind him an incredible record of original discovery in the whole
Pacific basin. And with him on this last voyage were some important
names in English exploration: George Vancouver, John Ledyard,
George Dixon, Nathaniel Portlock, Joseph Billings, and (as master
aboard the *Resolution*) William Bligh, later of *H.M.S. Bounty*. (Fire
Island near Anchorage was "discovered" by the stern disciplinarian
who, by mutiny, lost command of the *Bounty*.) Bligh, with Cook himself
and Vancouver, would rank high among the greatest navigators in the

history of sail. Cook's account of his visit is reported here from a three-volume work published in 1784, and entitled (believe it or not): *A Voyage to the Pacific Ocean. Undertaken, by the Command of His Majesty, for making Discoveries in the Northern Hemisphere. To determine the Position and Extent of the West Side of North America; its Distance from Asia; and the Practicability of a Northern Passage to Europe. Performed under the Direction of Captains COOK, CLERKE, AND GORE, In his Majesty's Ships the RESOLUTION and DISCOVERY. In the Years 1776, 1777, 1778, 1779 and 1780.*

M(onday, May 25, 1778) I intended going through one of the channels that divide . . . [the Barren Isles]; but meeting with a strong current setting against us, I bore up, and went to the leeward of them all. Toward the evening, the weather, which had been hazy all day, cleared up, and we got sight of a very lofty promontory, whose elevated summit, forming two exceedingly high mountains, was seen above the clouds. This promontory I named *Cape Douglas*, in honour of my very good friend, Dr. Douglas, canon of Windsor. . . .

Between this point and Cape Douglas, the coast seemed to form a large and deep bay; which, from some smoke that had been seen on Point Banks, obtained the name of *Smokey Bay*.

At day-break, the next morning, being the 26th, having got to the Northward of the Barren Isles, we discovered more land, extending from Cape Douglas to the North. It formed a chain of mountains of vast height; one of which, far more conspicuous than the rest, was named *Mount St. Augustin*. The discovery of this land did not discourage us; as it was supposed to be wholly unconnected with the land of Cape Elizabeth. For, in a North North East direction, the sight was unlimited by every thing but the horizon. We also thought, that there was a passage to the North West, between Cape Douglas and Mount St. Augustin. In short, it was imagined, that the land on our larboard, to the North of Cape Douglas, was composed of a group of islands, disjoined by so many channels, any

33

one of which we might make use of according as the wind should serve.

With these flattering ideas, having a fresh gale at North North East, we stood to the North West, till eight o'clock, when we clearly saw that what we had taken for islands were summits of mountains, every where connected by lower land, which the haziness of the horizon had prevented us from seeing at a greater distance. This land was every where covered with snow, from the tops of the hills down to the very sea-beach; and had every other appearance of being part of a great continent. I was now fully persuaded that I should find no passage by this inlet; and my persevering in the search of it here, was more to satisfy other people, than to confirm my own opinion.

* * *

(Saturday, 30) Until we got thus far [by tacking up the Inlet], the water had retained the same degree of saltness at low, as at high-water; and, at both periods, was as salt as that in the ocean. But now the marks of a river displayed themselves. The water taken up this ebb, when at the lowest, was found to be very considerably fresher, than any we had hitherto tasted; insomuch that I was convinced that we were in a large river, and not in a strait, communicating with the Northern seas. But as we had proceeded thus far, I was desirous of having stronger proofs; and, therefore, weighed with the next flood in the morning of the 31st, and plied higher up, or rather drove up with the tide; for we had but little wind.

About eight o'clock, we were visited by several of the natives, in one large, and several small canoes. The latter carried only one person each; and some had a paddle with a blade at each end, after the manner of the Esquimaux. In the large canoes were men, women, and children. Before they reached the ship, they displayed a leathern frock upon a long pole, as a sign, as we understood it, of their peaceable intentions. The frock they conveyed into the ship, in return for some trifles which I gave them. I could observe no difference between the persons, dress, ornaments, and boats of these people, and those of Prince William's Sound, except that the small canoes were rather of a less size, and carried only one man. We procured from them some of their fur dresses, made of the skins of sea-otters, martins, hares, and other animals; a few of their darts; and a small supply of salmon and halibut. In exchange for these they took old clothes, beads, and pieces of iron. We found that they were in possession of large iron knives, and of sky-blue glass beads, such as we had found amongst the natives of Prince William's Sound. These latter they seemed to value much, and consequently those which we now gave them. But their inclination led them, especially, to ask for large pieces of iron; which metal, if I was not much mistaken, they called by the name of *goone*; though, like their neighbours in Prince William's Sound, they seemed to have many significations to one word. They evidently spoke the same language; as the words *keeta*, *naema*, *oonaka*, and a few others of the most common we heard in that Sound, were also frequently used by this new tribe. After spending about two hours between the one ship and the other, they all retired to the Western shore.

At nine o'clock, we came to an anchor, in sixteen fathoms water, about two leagues from the West shore, and found the ebb already begun. At its greatest strength, it ran only three knots in the hour, and fell, upon a perpendicular, after we had anchored, twenty-one feet. The weather was misty, with drizzling rain, and clear, by turns. At the clear intervals, we saw an opening between the mountains on the Eastern shore, bearing East from the station of the ships, with low land, which we supposed to be islands lying between us and the main land. Low land was also seen to the Northward, that seemed to extend from the foot of the mountains on the one side, to those on the other; and, at low water, we perceived large shoals stretching out from this low land; some of which were at no great distance from us. From these appearances, we were in some doubt whether the inlet did not take an Easterly direction, through the above opening; or whether that opening was only a branch of it, and the main channel continued its Northern direction through the low land now in sight. The continuation and direction of the chain of mountains on each side of it, strongly indicated the probability of the latter supposition.

To determine this point, and to examine the shoals, I dispatched two boats, under the command of the master [Bligh]; and, as soon as the flood-tide made, followed with the ships: but, as it was a dead calm, and the tide strong, I anchored, after driving about ten miles in an East direction. At the lowest of the preceding ebb, the water at the surface, and for near a foot below it, was found to be perfectly fresh; retaining, however, a considerable degree of saltness at a greater depth. Besides this, we had now many other, and but too evident, proofs of being in a great river. Such as low shores; very thick and muddy water; large trees, and all manner of dirt and rubbish, floating up and down with the tide. In the afternoon, the natives, in several canoes, paid us another visit; and trafficked with our people for some time, without ever giving us reason to accuse them of any act of dishonesty.

At two o'clock next morning, being the 1st of June, the master returned, and reported that he found the inlet, or rather, river, contracted to the breadth of one league, by low land on each side, through which it took a Northerly direction. He proceeded three leagues through this narrow part, which he found navigable for the largest ships, being from twenty to seventeen fathoms deep. The least water, at a proper distance from the shore and shoals, was ten fathoms; and this was before he entered the narrow part. While the ebb or stream run down, the water was perfectly fresh; but, after the flood made, it became brackish; and, toward high water, very much so, even as high up as he went. He landed upon an island, which lies between this branch and the Eastern one; and upon it saw some currant bushes, with the fruit already set; and some other fruit-trees and bushes, unknown to him. The soil appeared to be clay, mixed with sand. About three leagues beyond the extent of his search, or to the Northward of it, he observed there was another separation in the Eastern chain of mountains, through which he supposed the river took a North East direction; but it seemed rather more probable that this was only another branch, and that the main channel kept its Northern direction, between the two ridges or chains of mountains before mentioned. . . .

All hopes of finding a passage were now given up. But as the ebb was almost spent, and we could not return against the flood, I thought I might as well take the advantage of the latter, to get a nearer view of the Eastern branch; and, by that means, finally to determine whether the low land on the East side of the river was an island, as we had supposed, or not. With this purpose in view, we weighed with the first of the flood, and, having a faint breeze at North East, stood over for the Eastern shore, with boats ahead, sounding. Our depth was from twelve to five fathoms; the bottom a hard gravel, though the water was exceedingly muddy. At eight o'clock, a fresh breeze sprung up at East, blowing in an opposite direction to our course; so that I despaired of reaching the entrance of the river, to which we were plying up, before high-water. But thinking that what the ships could not do, might be done by boats, I dispatched two, under the command of Lieutenant King, to examine the tides, and to make such other observations as might give us some insight into the nature of the river.

At ten o'clock, finding the ebb begun, I anchored in nine fathoms water, over a gravelly bottom. Observing the tide to be too strong for the boats to make head against it, I made a signal for them to return on board, before they had got half way to the entrance of the river they were sent to examine, which bore from us South 80° East, three leagues distant. The principal information gained by this tide's work, was the determining that all the low land, which we had supposed to be an island or islands, was one continued tract, from the banks of the great river, to the foot of the mountains, to which it joined; and that it terminated at the South entrance of this Eastern branch, which I shall distinguish by the name of *River Turnagain*. On the North side of this river, the low land again begins, and stretches out from the foot of the mountains, down to the banks of the great river; so that, before the river Turnagain, it forms a large bay, on the South side of which we were now at anchor; and where we had from twelve to five fathoms, from half-flood to high-water. . . .

If the discovery of this great river [or inlet, called by Lord Sandwich, *Cook's River*], which promises to vie with the most considerable ones already known to be capable of extensive inland navigation, should prove of use either to the present, or to any future age, the time we spent in it ought to be the less regretted. But to us, who had a much greater object in view, the delay thus occasioned was an essential loss. The season was advancing apace. We knew not how far we might have to proceed to the South; and we were now convinced, that the continent of North America extended farther to the West, than, from the modern most reputable charts, we had reason to expect. This made the existence of a passage into Baffin's or Hudson's Bays less probable; or, at least, shewed it to be of greater extent. It was a satisfaction to me, however, to reflect, that, if I had not examined this very considerable inlet, it would have been assumed, by speculative fabricators of geography, as a fact, that it communicated with the sea to the North, or with Baffin's or Hudson's Bay to the East; and been marked, perhaps, on future maps of the world, with greater precision, and more certain signs of reality, than the invisible, because imaginary, Straits of de Fuca, and de Fonte.

In the afternoon, I sent Mr. King again, with two armed boats, with orders to land, on the Northern point of the low land, on the South East side of the river; there to display the flag; to take possession of the country and river, in his Majesty's name; and to bury in the ground a bottle, containing some pieces of English coin, of the year 1772, and a paper, on which was inscribed the names of our ships, and the date of our discovery. In the mean time, the ships were got under sail, in order to proceed down the river. The wind still blue fresh, Easterly; but a calm ensued, not long after we were under way; and the flood-tide meeting us off the point where Mr. King landed (and which thence got the name of *Point Possession*), we were obliged to drop anchor in six fathoms water, with the point bearing South, two miles distant.

When Mr. King returned, he informed me, that as he approached the shore, about twenty of the natives made their appearance, with their arms extended; probably, to express thus their peaceable disposition, and to shew that they were without weapons. On Mr. King's, and the gentlemen with him, landing, with musquets in their hands, they seemed alarmed, and made signs expressive of their request to lay them down. This was accordingly done; and then they suffered the gentlemen to walk up to them, and appeared to be cheerful and sociable. They had with them a few pieces of fresh salmon, and several dogs. Mr. Law, surgeon of the Discovery, who was one of the party, having bought one of the latter, took it down toward the boat, and shot it dead, in their sight. This seemed to surprize them exceedingly; and, as if they did not think themselves safe in such company, they walked away; but it was soon after discovered, that their spears, and other weapons, were hid in the bushes close behind them. Mr. King also informed me, that the ground was swampy, and the soil poor, light, and black. It produced a few trees and shrubs; such as pines, alders, birch, and willows; rose and currant bushes; and a little grass; but they saw not a single plant in flower.

6

The Promised Land in 1786

by William Beresford

... her complexion and features [were] far from disagreeable: indeed I have often seen much worse-looking women in England.

C aptain Cook wrote: "There is not the least doubt, that a very beneficial fur trade might be carried on with the inhabitants of this vast coast. But unless a Northern passage should be found practicable, it seems rather too remote for Great Britain to receive any emolument from it." Despite Cook's remark, two of his own men—Nathaniel Portlock and George Dixon—were sent to the North Pacific on the *King George* and the *Queen Charlotte*, by a British trading company, the year after publication of Cook's *Voyage*. The Russians were already in Cook Inlet. In letters home dated July and August 1786, William Beresford, aboard the *Queen Charlotte*, described the encounter with Russian and native traders.

At eleven o'clock in the forenoon of the 19th [July], we made the entrance of Cook's River, leaving the Barren Isles to the Southward and Eastward. Both wind and tide being now in our favour, we kept standing along the Eastern shore, intending, if possible, to make Anchor Point before we let go our anchor; but at seven in the afternoon we were surprized with the report of a gun, which proceeded from a bay nearly a-breast of us, at about four miles distance. Captain Portlock immediately fired a gun, by way of answering this signal, and there being every appearance of a good harbour, he determined to stand in, and come to anchor, in order that we might know what nation had got the start of us.

Various were our conjectures on this head; some thinking they might possibly be our own countrymen; others, that they were French; and indeed this latter conjecture had a good deal of weight with us, as we had heard of two French ships fitting out for this coast, at the time we left England. However, all our surmises were soon changed into certainty, for as we were standing into the bay with a light breeze, a boat came from the shore to the King George, and the people proved to be Russians. . . .

It seems the Russians had no fixed settlement here, and, in short, no other residence than a mere temporary one, which they had made by hauling their boats on shore, and laying them on their beam-ends, with skins drawn fore and aft, to shelter them from the inclemency of the weather. All that could be learnt from them was, that they came in a sloop from Onalaska, and that the people we had seen in the canoes were Codiac Indians, which they had brought with them, the better to facilitate their traffic with the inhabitants of Cook's River, and the adjacent country; but notwithstanding this, they had frequently quarelled and fought with the natives, and were at present on such bad terms with them, that they never went to sleep without their arms ready loaded by their side. However, the accounts we got seldom agreed, and gave us but an indifferent idea of their proceedings, though this might arise, in a great measure, from our having but a very imperfect knowledge of the Russian language: thus much we were pretty certain of, that they had met with very few, if any skins, though they had got nankeens, and Persian silks to traffic with.

The watering place here is so very convenient, that we compleated our water in one day, viz. the 21st: from that to the 26th, the people were employed in cutting wood, and recreating themselves on shore.

On the 24th, our Captains went to survey the bay, and landing on the South East point, they found a vein of coals, some of which were brought on board. The bay, from this circumstance, obtained the name of Coal Harbour.

Our people frequently tried to catch fish with a hook and line, but to no purpose: however, Captain Portlock having a seine on board, it was frequently hauled with success, and large quantities of fine salmon caught, which were generally divided between the ships.

The country here is very mountainous: the hills sloping down nearest the shore, are totally covered with pines, intermixed with birch, alder, and various other trees and shrubs, whilst the more distant mountains, whose lofty summits outreach the clouds, are totally covered with snow, and have the appearance of everlasting Winter. But I shall not at present attempt any farther description of a country, which as yet I am so little acquainted with: let it suffice for thee at present to know, that though this is the latter end of July, the weather is in general cold, damp, and disagreeable, with frequent showers of snow or sleet; and the surrounding prospect barren, dreary, and uncomfortable. So much at present for the *promised land*.

* * *

By our observation to-day [July 28] at noon, the place where we now lay is in 60 deg. 48 min. North latitude; and 152 deg. 11 min. West longitude. From this to the 3rd of August, the weather was moderate and fine: our friends [the natives] kept bringing us skins of various kinds, but gave us to understand, that their own were all sold, and that they were obliged to trade with tribes in distant parts of the country, in order to supply us. They also brought us great plenty of excellent fresh salmon, which we bought very cheap, giving a single bead for a large fish; indeed they were so plentiful, that at any time if we refused to purchase, they would throw the fish on board, sooner than be at the pains to take them back. The salmon come into the river in innumerable shoals, at this season of the year, and are caught by the natives in wears, with the greatest ease; they are smoaked and dried in their huts, and make a very considerable part of their food during the Winter. What a fresh instance this of the goodness of Divine Providence towards his creatures! How bountifully he hath provided for these poor wretches, in this barren and inhospitable part of the world! Surely, after this, no one can ask with the discontented Israelites, "Can God spread a table in the wilderness?" . . .

Before I proceed farther, let me endeavor to give thee some idea of the country near the place we now lay; and surely a prospect more dreary and uncomfortable can scarcely be conceived, than that which presented itself to our view to the North West. The land, indeed, close by the sea-side, is tolerably level, affords a few pines, which, together with shrubs and underwoods, intermixed with long grass, make the landscape not altogether disagreeable; but the adjacent mountains, whose rugged tops far outreach the clouds, absolutely beggar all description: covered with eternal snow, except where the fierce North wind blows it from their craggy summits, they entirely chill the blood of the beholder, and their prodigious extent and stupendous precipices, render them equally inaccessible to man or beast. I had forgot, that in my last I promised to attempt no more descriptions of the country at present, but the prospect just mentioned had something in it so awfully dreadful, that I could not avoid saying a few words respecting it, and I know thou wilt readily forgive any little inadvertencies of this sort, as my only wish is, to amuse and entertain—I wish I could add, and instruct thee. . . .

* * *

In regard to the extent of this river, I cannot speak with any degree of certainty; but we know that it reaches considerably farther to the Northward than where we lay at anchor. With respect to its breadth, it is seldom more than twenty miles over.

The inhabitants seem not to have fixed on any particular spot for their residence, but are scattered about here and there, as best suits their convenience or inclination. 'Tis most probable they are divided into clans or tribes, as in every large canoe we saw there was at least one person of superior authority to the rest, who not only directed their traffic, but kept them in a proper degree of subordination. In their manners they seem harmless and inoffensive; but this might probably be occasioned by the different treatment they met with from us, to what the Russians had used them to. The weapons we saw are bows and arrows, and spears; these are very useful in hunting, as well as fighting; the flesh of the various beasts they kill serving them for food, as their skins do for cloathing. One would reasonably suppose that the skins of large beasts, as bears, wolves, &c. would be held in the greatest estimation as cloaths by these people: this, however, is not the case, the greater part wearing cloaks made of marmot-skins, very neatly sewed together, one cloak containing perhaps more than one hundred skins: it is most likely that their women's time is principally taken up in employments like these. . . .

In their persons, these people are of a middle size, and well proportioned; their features appear regular, but their faces are so bedaubed with dirt and filth, that it is impossible to say what sort of complexion they have. That person seems to be reckoned the greatest beau amongst them, whose face is one entire piece of smut and grease, and his hair well daubed with the same composition. Their nose and ears are ornamented with beads, or teeth, if they cannot procure any thing else: they have likewise a long slit cut in the upper lip, parallel with the mouth, which is ornamented much in the same manner with the nose and ears; but this I could observe was always in proportion to the person's wealth. We saw only one woman, and the people with her behaved with great civility, and attended her with great respect: her face, contrary to the general custom, was tolerably clean, and her complexion and features far from disagreeable: indeed I have often seen much worse-looking women in England. . . .

7

Foreign Greed & Cupidity, 1786-1790

by I. A. Pill

... the foreigners, eager themselves to avoid military action, would cruise or try to cruise in waters where they thought they would be able to conceal from our subjects the consequences of their greed and cupidity. ...

The Russians in Alaska did not welcome the poaching foreigners. After Bering, *promyshlenniki* (fur hunters and traders) island-hopped along the Aleutians eastward, and in 1784 the Shelekhov/Golikov Company founded a permanent settlement on Kodiak Island, below the mouth of Cook Inlet. Two years later the same firm established a post called Alexandrovsk on the mainland at English Bay. A rival company of the merchant Lebedev-Lastochkin founded Fort St. George at Kasilof, probably in the following year, then in 1791, Nikolaevsk Redoubt at Kenai. Judging from the report of Governor-General Pil of Irkutsk, to Tsarina Catherine, both firms were harrassed by the English and Spanish. The report is dated February 14, 1790.

*T*o Her Most Serene Majesty, the Most Powerful, Great Empress Yekaterina Alekseyevna, Ruler of All the Russians, Most Gracious Majesty, from the Lieutenant-General, Governor-General of Irkutsk and Kolyvan, and Knight

The tireless efforts and the audacity of the Europeans in competing with Russia for the hunting-posts and the trade along the shores of the Northeastern Ocean, which are the sole possession of the Russians, have not been limited to the partial success of the East India Company, but have given additional impetus to their progress—in spite of all the difficulties they have encountered—to the very depths of North America, where the Russian hunters and traders are only now beginning to attain the aim which has been the main object of their intentions, namely, the utilization to the full of the hunting and the trading with the savage islanders that have newly been established and have proved very successful. The intensification of their operations in those waters while they leave behind them all the signs of considerable plundering of the wealth of that region, proves the substantial nature of their activities and brings to the fore the methods by which all the benefits of our seafarers will be taken away from them, and which will tend to create for them nothing but toil and vexation.

In my first report to Your Majesty on this matter I took the liberty of describing to Your Imperial Majesty the efforts made by

47

the Company of the two noted citizens, Golikov of Kursk and Shelekhov of Rylsk, along the American coast, pointing out the fact that the portion of the mainland explored by them together with other islands had become the possession of the Russian nation. In this report I hope, Most Gracious Majesty, that it will please you to find my deposition on the past activities of the European vessels which were plying the seas in various parts of America and along the coasts of the islands. On entering upon my task I regard it my absolute duty not to pass over in silence before Your Majesty that the Russian fur-hunters and traders, when they directed their exploration to that part of the vast ocean, in spite of their not so enviable success managed, nevertheless, by means of their friendly attitude alone toward the islanders, to establish such useful cooperation with them that the attempts of the Europeans—many of which utilized armed vessels—were restrained from trying to attain the direct goal of their undertaking. The Russians did not dare, of course, to arm themselves against the Europeans, not because they were afraid of them but because the foreigners, eager themselves to avoid military action, would cruise or try to cruise in waters where they thought they would be able to conceal from our subjects the consequences of their greed and cupidity and their intentions on that score.

The penetration of the English and the Spaniards to the shores of the Kuriles and the Aleutian Islands and to the coast of America itself can now be admitted to Your Majesty as one of the most daring undertakings of those two powers, since it aims at throwing down the gauge of competition in areas which, by the right of first discovery by Your expeditions, should be regarded as completely outside the scope of their activities; inasmuch as those seafarers, having thrown aside all fear, have by this time strengthened themselves among the savage tribes to such a degree that the trade in furs and hunting itself are now in their hands, giving affront to the rights of Your empire. Therefore I hasten, Most August Majesty, to continue the account of the reasons that prompted me to submit the present report. . . .

1. Master Izmaylov, of the company of Golikov and Shelekhov reports on March 1, [1]788 that on his way by galliot from the Okhotsk roadstead to North America across the strait separating the Kuriles from the Aleutian Islands, was informed upon reaching the island of Kodiak, by the fur-hunters there, that during the year

[1]786 two large ships described as English had put in at Kenai Gulf [or, Cook Inlet], and that two others were cruising around off shore in plain sight of Kodiak itself. Upon the oncoming of the winter of [1]787 three additional ships came to anchor in Chugach territory and one yawl engaged in trade with the Kenai tribes. This yawl, when it started on the return trip to Chugach territory, was supposed to have lost five men to a Chugach attack and to have been compelled to leave two more men to the Chugaches in absolute captivity. Then there seemed to be another ship in those waters, but since fate did not smile upon it either, all its men were exposed to death at the hands of the islanders and it finally fell a prey to the flames. The last incident and the supposed burning of the abovementioned yawl by the savages are not confirmed by Master Izmaylov, but everything else he gives out as really probable, since many of the Russian workmen paid more than one visit to the boats which found shelter in Kenai Gulf.

2nd. Master Becharov, who served in the same company, on February 28, [1]789 tells almost the same story as Izmaylov. He maintains that when the foreign ships put out to sea, the Russians no longer had left even a particle of the trade which they might have been able to secure with the islanders; since the foreigners in exchanging their goods for American merchandise, were interested only in adding to their profits. The same Bocharov explains that the English, by striking out greedily to obtain fur-bearing animals, spurred on our fur-hunters to answer them with a letter by special messenger in the hope that the Russians would also try to win them over in the guise of wanting to do business with them. Becoming aware, however, from the exchange that the Russians were subjects of Your Majesty and not some native tribe, they immediately pushed off to sea with the greatest of haste.

3rd. The head of this Company, our agent the Greek Dalarov reports of April 28 of last year that in the month of May, [1]788, in the so-called Kenai Gulf which is also known as Grossefluss there appeared a foreign vessel, a two-master, which rode at anchor for about six days and then, after an open letter had been delivered from it to Dalarov, put to sea. Later, in June and July again two boats came, one putting in at the island of Shelidak and the other at the island of Tugidak. They made presents to the islanders of various European articles, and distributed silver medals among them. That same agent asserts that those two ships were Spanish, inasmuch as he, speaking to their commander who called himself captain and to the officers under him, was not only convinced of it but even received information from them that led him to believe that they might have been proceeding from Acapulco to the North Chukotsk sea. Wherefore those navigators handed to the Russians on the island of Tugidak a sealed letter in the name of one of the ministers for overseas Indian affairs, Don Antonio Valdez. And Dalarov submitted separately six open letters, together with three of the aforementioned medals, which he had obtained from the islanders by exchange. At the end of those reports it is explained that the Kenai natives, evidently beguiled by the visit that the foreigners paid them, became so bold as to try to exterminate the Russian traders. First they killed ten of the Golikov and Shelekhov Company in Alaska, then, in another place, they put to death four workmen of another company, that of the merchant Lebedev-Lastochkin of Yakutsk. . . .

8

Trade War in the Late 18th Century

by A. A. Baranov

*It hurts me to see [the natives] robbed and made prisoners
by men of our own race and creed. What's more, in
time they could be useful for our business up north.*

Foreign competition in the Cook Inlet area was minor and
temporary and did not seriously disrupt the Russian trade. More
significant for the efficient pursuit of the region's peltry was a fierce
rivalry between two Russian firms: the Lebedev-Lastochkin company
and the Shelekhov/Golikov firm. In 1799 the latter received a monopoly
of all of Alaska's business, as the Russian American Company, but only
after its dynamic manager, Alexandr Baranov, confronted and dealt
forcibly with his chief rival in Cook Inlet. In Baranov's report to Georgii
Shelekhov, dated July 24, 1793, some of the nastier aspects of the
competition are detailed. Shelekhov himself was doubtless unper-
turbed by the struggle; he owned shares in both companies.

*N*ow I will explain to you our troubles with Lebedev's Company. After Konovalov was sent away, they with their two ships, the *Ioann* and the *George* tried to do as much harm to our Company as possible. Trying to force us out, their first aim was to make us abandon . . . [Cook Inlet]. They took possession of . . . [Kachemak Bay], and settled a big *artel* there. They didn't let us trap foxes, even though our cabin still stood as proof that we were there first. I enclose a copy of an agreement in which Kolomin states that along with other ground, this bay is our territory. In their locality, they made real slaves of the natives and forbade them to have any communication with us. Then they sent an order to me at Kodiak signed by Kolomin, Konovalov, Balushin, skipper Zaikov, and a certain Samoilov to claim that according to some official document, of which I never saw either the original nor a copy, all . . . [Cook Inlet] belonged to them. They ordered us to get out, and forbade us to get furs there. It was the same with . . . [Prince William Sound]. . . . I was told by Kenai natives . . . that Balushin and Kolomin, with six baidaras, were awaiting Galaktionov's return from Kodiak for a chance to attack our Kenai crew, chase our men to Kodiak, and subjugate the [Aleut] and Kenai natives dependent on them. They were waiting only for his return to start hostilities with all their forces against our company.

I finally received from Malakhov, at Kenai, a confirmation of this bad news. Numbering 60 Russians and several natives, they actually are staying not far from our crew. They have already begun hostilities, beating the men in two of our hunting parties, one under the command of Kotelnikov, sent with 40 baidarkas to hunt sea otters, and the other under Larionov with 8 baidarkas. They took from the natives their baidarkas, hunting darts and seal skins, beat them up and crippled some of them. Those who could not flee they tied up, threw them in their baidaras, and took them along. They then tried to deny us [Prince William Sound]. . . .

On the north side of Aliaksa they committed the following dastardly deed: out of the four villages I had annexed in the name of the Empress, they plundered two and took the people prisoners. They took the crest of State which I had given to a chief and threw it on the ground and broke it. They said that this crest was a children's toy and that I was just fooling people. The chief who came from there told me all that in the presence of Galaktionov, who signed as a witness. The perpetrator of these crimes is a certain Irkutsk townsman, Alexander Ivanov.

The Company is getting very little profit from these natives, leaving them complete freedom. Only once in a while they bring a few otter and deer skins because they don't know how to hunt the sea animals and there isn't much game in the mountains. Still they should have protection. They are our allies, were annexed by us, and they thought that we were going to see to their safety. It hurts me to see them robbed and made prisoners by men of our own race and creed. What's more, in time they could be useful for our business up north. I am forwarding to the commandant at Okhotsk the census of them together with the census of the Chugach natives, and all the papers concerning the harmful activities of Lebedev's men. You can take copies of them there and look through them and ask for a decision. . . .

9

An Unpleasant Visit to Kenai in 1794

by George Vancouver

... we should not have been inclined to have partaken of the repast, in a place, where the atmosphere we inhaled was so extremely offensive, that every sensation that is unpleasant was excited, excepting that of hunger.

Still another English scientific expedition entered Cook Inlet, on Saturday April 12, 1794, this one commanded by Captain George Vancouver. His cartographic survey took one month, during which time the two northern arms of the bay were investigated closely, new geographical names were added to the landscape, and "Cook's River" became "Cook's Inlet." Mr. Whidbey, in a boat from Vancouver's flagship *Discovery*, searched in vain for the bottle buried on Point Possession by the Cook expedition. It has never been recovered.

Vancouver and his men made detailed observations of the countryside, and the Captain had many good things to say about the natives' character and deportment. He thought less well of the Russians' life-style, judging from his description of a visit to Kenai.

Soon after we had anchored, the commanding officer at the place sent a very civil message, requesting we would visit their habitation, with which after breakfast, accompanied by Mr. Menzies and our Russian passenger, I complied. As we drew near to the shore the depth of water gradually decreased, until in the entrance of the creek we found but one fathom from side to side. On our arrival here we were saluted by two guns from a kind of balcony, above which the Russian flag was displayed on the top of a house situated on the cliffs, which in most places compose the shores of the upper part of the inlet, rising perpendicularly from a beach, which generally commences at high water mark.

The compliment of two guns was repeated on our landing, where we met some Russians, who came to welcome and conduct us to their dwelling by a very indifferent path, which was rendered more disagreeable by a most intolerable stench, the worst, excepting that of the skunk, I had ever the inconvenience of experiencing; occasioned I believe by a deposit made during the winter of an immense collection of all kinds of filth, offal, &c. that had now become a fluid mass of putrid matter, just without the railing that inclosed the Russian factory, over which these noxious exhalations spread, and seemed to become a greater nuisance by their combination with the effluvia arising from the houses.

We were however constrained to pass some time in this establishment, which occupied a space of about an hundred and twenty yards square, fenced in by a very stout paling of small spars of pine and birch, placed close together about twelve feet high. These were fixed firm in the ground, yet they appeared to be a very defenceless barricade against any hostile attempts, even of the Indians, as the whole might easily be reduced to ashes by fire on the outside, as could also their houses within the fence, those being built with wood and covered with thatch. The largest of these, resembling in its shape a barn, was about thirty-five yards long, about as many feet in breadth, and about ten or twelve feet high; this was appropriated to the residence of thirty-six Russians, who, with their commander Mr. Stephen Zikoff, then on an excursion to Prince William's sound, comprehended the total number of Russians at this station; all of whom excepting the commander reside in this house, which principally consists of one common room, answering all the purposes of shelter, feeding, and sleeping in. For their better accommodation when at rest, two platforms, each about eight feet wide, were raised about eight or nine inches from the ground or floor, and extended from end to end on each side of the room; these were divided into eighteen open partitions or stalls, one of which was allotted to each person, as his particular apartment, the middle of the room being common to them all. The stalls were divided like those in the stables of public inns, by posts only, on which hung their spare apparel, with their arms and accoutrements. The room though unglazed was tolerably light, as in the windows a substitute for glass was made use of, which we supposed to be a thin membrane from the intestines of the whale; this admitted a sufficient quantity of light for all their purposes, and excluded the wind and inclemency of the weather. The largest of these windows was at the furthest or upper end, near which stood a very humble wooden table very rudely wrought, and surrounded by forms of the same material.

To these we were conducted by two of the party who seemed to have some superiority over the rest, one of whom appeared to be the principal person in the absence of Mr. Zikoff, the other a kind of steward or person charged with the moveable property belonging to the factory. If we understood them right this settlement had been thus established twelve years, notwithstanding which we did not perceive that any attempt had been made either to cultivate the land, or to supply themselves more comfortably by the introduction of domestic animals. The only refreshment they had to offer, was some cold boiled halibut, and raw dried salmon intended to be eaten with it by way of bread. This very homely fare produced us no disappointment; for had it been otherways, and consisting of the greatest niceties, we should not have been inclined to have partaken of the repast, in a place, where the atmosphere we inhaled was so extremely offensive, that every sensation that is unpleasant was excited, excepting that of hunger.

This occasioned the shortening of our visit as much as common civility would allow, and as we prepared to seek the relief of a purer air, we were attended by our two leaders in taking a view of the rest of the settlement. We found it to consist of a smaller house situated at the west end of the large one, in which Mr. Zikoff the commander resided, and two or three and twenty others of different dimensions all huddled together without any kind of regularity, appropriated to the depositing of stores, and to the educating of Indian children in the Russian language and religious persuasion; they were also the residence of such of the natives as were the companions, or the immediate attendants on the Russians composing the establishment. Our attention was next directed to the vessel we had been informed belonged to this place. She was found hauled up just above the general line of high water mark, close under the cliffs on which their houses were erected. Her burthen I estimated at about sixty or seventy tons; she was very clumsily rigged with two masts, and her hull had the oakum dropping out of the seams, and was in other respects much out of repair. In this situation she had been for two years, and was still to remain there two years longer, when this party would be relieved, and the vessel repaired, in which they would return to Kamtschatka.

The place where the vessel was laid up was hardly within sight of their habitation, she could therefore in the event of any misunderstanding with the natives have been easily set on fire, or otherwise destroyed, which could not have been so easily accomplished had she remained in the creek, where the water seemed to be of sufficient depth to keep her constantly afloat, and by that means to afford the Russians a retreat that might prove very desirable in the event of any insurrection. Their apprehensions however on this score did not seem very great, for they were very ill provided to defend themselves against any attack. The whole of their armour consisted of two small brass swivel guns, each carrying about a pound shot, mounted on the balcony at the top of the large house, which is sufficiently high to overlook all the inclosed premises; a similar piece of ordnance at the door of the entrance, about a dozen muskets hanging apparently in constant readiness near the upper end of the great room, with two or three pistols, and a few short daggers.

Our curiosity and inquiries thus satisfied, I invited these two gentlemen to accompany us on board, with which they readily complied. They presented me with a few skins of the land animals found in the neighbourhood, and a very fine halibut, which was highly acceptable, as it was the first fresh fish we had procured this season. A brisk northerly breeze prevailed on our reaching the ship; this temptation to proceed was too great to allow of our remaining at anchor, though it necessarily shortened the stay of our visitors. On their departure I gave them a small assortment of such things as were most likely to prove serviceable in their retirement, which they very thankfully accepted.

10

The Tragic Case of the Fallen Monk (1796-?)

by H. H. Bancroft

. . . when they were told that I had come among them to make better men of them, one of them, named Katlewah, the brother of a chief, said he was glad of that, as they had many bad men among the Iliamna people, especially his brother.

About the time that Vancouver was charting the Inlet, a few monks of the Russian Church arrived in Alaska to Christianize the natives and minister to the traders. One was sainted recently. Another, Father Juvenal, was martyred while performing his missionary work in the Iliamna region. The detailed story of his fate, as reported by Hubert Howe Bancroft in 1886, was drawn from what purports to be a translation of Juvenal's diary, now in Bancroft Library of the University of California at Berkeley. The "diary" is almost certainly an invention, although its fraudulence may never be established conclusively. Ivan Petroff, a Russian immigrant who worked for Bancroft, "translated" the journal; the "original" was somehow lost. The dramatic account is reprinted here as an early example of historical fiction set in the Cook Inlet area.

After a tedious passage from island to island, sometimes meeting with long delays, the priest reached the ... Kenai River, where was the nearest station of the Lebedef Company, on the 11th of August [1796]. Here, notwithstanding Baranof's warning, he met with the first signs of religious observance by promyshleniki during his travels in the colonies. During his stay of about a fortnight he married several couples, baptized a number of infants and adults, and at intervals held divine service, which was well attended.

Soon, however, the religious ardor cooled, and so little interest did the natives take in the missionary that, when ready to depart, he found it difficult to obtain men and bidarkas to take him across the inlet to his destination. At last one morning after service he appealed to the natives for men to assist him across the water, telling them that he must go to the Ilyamna country to preach the new word to the people, who had never yet heard it. Thereupon an old man arose and remarked that he ought not to go; that the Kenaitze people had been friends of the Russians for long years, and had a better right to have a priest among them than the Ilyamnas, who were very bad. The missionary, in his journal, confessed that he was puzzled for a fitting reply to this argument. On the 25th, however, he set out from the station, accompanied by two men from Chekituk village.

A delay was again occasioned by his guides indulging in a seal-hunt on Kalgin Island, situated midway in the inlet, and the western shore was not reached till the 29th. On the 30th he writes: "This morning two natives came out of the forest and shouted to my companions. Two of the latter went out to meet them. There was a great deal of talking before the strangers concluded to come to our tents. When they came at last, and I was pointed out to them as the man who was to live among them, they wished to see my goods. I encountered some difficulty in making them understand that I am not here to trade and barter, and have nothing for sale. Finally, when they were told that I had come among them to make better men of them, one of them, named Katlewah, the brother of a chief, said he was glad of that, as they had many bad men among the Ilyamna people, especially his brother. The two savages have agreed to carry my chattels for me to their village, but, to satisfy Katlewah, I was compelled to open every bundle and show him the contents. I did not like the greedy glitter in his eye when he saw and felt of my vestments."

On the 3d of September the party reached Ilyamna village, after a fatiguing journey over the mountains and a canoe voyage on the lake. Shakmut, the chief, received the missionary with friendly words, interpreted by a boy named Nikita, who had been a hostage with the Russians. He invited him to his own house, and on the priest's expressing a wish for a separate residence, promised to have one built for him, and allowed him to retain Nikita in his service. Finding that the latter, though living with the Russians for years, had not been baptized, Juvenal performed that ceremony at the first opportunity, before the astonished natives, who regarded it as sorcery, and one asked whether Nikita would live many days.

Juvenal's success was not remarkable, to judge from his diary. One young woman asked to be baptized like the boy Nikita, expressing the hope that then she could also live in the new house with the missionary. An old woman brought two boys, stating that they were orphans who had nobody to care for them, and that she would like to see them baptized, "to change their luck." The chief Shakmut also promised to consider the question of embracing Christianity, and for some reason he did so promise in the presence of the whole tribe, and amidst great feasting and rejoicing. Two servants and one of his wives were included in the ceremony, the priest not daring to refuse them on the ground that they had received no instructions, for fear of losing the advantage which the chief's example might give him in his future work.

The conversion of the chief had not, however, the desired effect; it only led to dissensions among the people, and when the priest began to tell the converts that they must put away their secondary wives, the chief and others began to plot his downfall. It had been a marvel to the savages that a man should put a bridle upon his passions and live in celibacy, but their wonder was mingled with feelings of respect. To overcome the influence which the missionary was gaining over some of his people, Shakmut, or Alexander as he was now christened, plotted to throw temptation in his way, and alas for Juvenal! whose priestly wrath had been so lately roused by the immorality of Baranof and his godless crew of promyshleniki, it must be related that he fell. In the dead of night, according to his own confession, an Ilyamna damsel captured him by storm.

On the day after this incident, the outraged ecclesiastic received a visit from Katlewah, who expressed a wish to be baptized on the following sabbath. "I can tell by his manner," writes the priest on September 26th, "that he knows of my disgrace, though he did not say anything. When I walked to the forest to-day to cut some wood, I heard two girls laughing at me, behind my back; and in the morning, when I was making a wooden bolt for the door of my sleeping-room, a woman looked in and laughed right into my face. She may be the one who caused my fall, for it was dark and I never saw her countenance. Alexander visited me, also, and insisted upon having his wives baptized next Sunday. I had no spirit left to contest the matter with him, and consented; but I shall not shrink from my duty to make him relinquish all but one wife when the proper time arrives. If I wink at polygamy now, I shall be forever unable to combat it. Perhaps it is only imagination, but I think I can discover a lack of respect in Nikita's behavior toward me since yesterday." Continuing his journal on the 27th, he adds: "My disgrace has become public already, and I am laughed at wherever I go, especially by the women. Of course they do not understand the sin, but rather look upon it as a good joke. It will require great firmness on my part to regain what respect I have lost for myself as well as on behalf of the church. I have vowed to burn no fuel in my bedroom during the whole winter, in order to chastise my body—a mild punishment, indeed, compared to the blackness of my sin."

The next day was Sunday. "With a heavy heart," says Juvenal, "but with a firm purpose, I baptized Katlewah and his family, the three wives of the chief, seven children, and one aged couple. Under any other circumstances such a rich harvest would have filled me with joy, but I am filled with gloom." In the evening he called on Alexander and found him and his wives carousing together. Notwithstanding his recent downfall, the priest's wrath was kindled, and through Nikita he informed the chief that he must marry one of his wives according to the rites of the church, and put away the rest, or be forever damned. Alexander now became angry in his turn and bade him leave the house. On his way home he met Katlewah, who rated him soundly, declaring that he had lied to them all, for "his brother was as bad as ever, and no good had come of any of his baptisms."

The career of Father Juvenal was now ended, and the little that remains to be said is best told in his own words: "September 29th. The chief and his brother have both been here this morning and abused me shamefully. Their language I could not understand, but they spat in my face, and what was worse, upon the sacred images on the walls. Katlewah seized my vestments and carried them off, and I was left bleeding from a blow struck with an ivory club by the chief. Nikita has bandaged and washed my wounds; but from his anxious manner I can see that I am still in danger. The other boys have run away. My wound pains me so that I can scarcely—" Here the manuscript journal breaks off, and probably the moment after the last line was penned his assassins entered and completed their work by stabbing him to the heart. This at least was his fate, as represented by the boy Nikita, who escaped with the diary and other papers to a Russian settlement, and delivered them into the hands of Father Veniaminof on his first visit to the Nushegak villages.

11

Remarks About The Occurrence of Gold, 1848-1855

by Petr Doroshin

*We obtained color immediately . . . and the more we
climbed into the valley the more we perceived clearly
that still larger flakes were always evident the farther we
hiked from our starting place.*

Fur hunting by the Russians continued in the area on a small
scale, even after the Russian American Company moved its
headquarters from Kodiak to Sitka at the turn of the century. By 1850,
new agricultural settlements of former Company employees had been
founded at Seldovia, Ninilchik and Eklutna (called Knik). A few
attempts were made to explore the region; they rarely extended very
far inland. At least one expedition attempted to ascend the Susitna
River (spelled "Sushitna" in the early documents but cleaned up later
by people whose passion for public decency exceeded their devotion to
historical accuracy). I. G. Voznesenskii, a collector for the Imperial

Academy of Sciences, examined the natural history of the area in 1842-1843.

An important investigation was made in the mid-nineteenth century by a mining engineer sent to search for minerals. The engineer, Petr Doroshin, found gold on the Kenai River about the same time that James Marshall noticed the precious metal at Sutter's Mill in California, but no Forty-niners rushed to Cook Inlet. However, Doroshin's report on the coal at Port Graham, mentioned by Portlock, resulted in the construction of a mine there. In the following document, Doroshin summarizes his activity and discusses the failure of Russia and the Company to follow up his discovery of gold.

*I*n 1850 I was sent to Cook Inlet to search more closely for gold, which I had already found in small quantities during my first visit to the colonies in 1848 (before the discovery of gold in California had been reported in Sitka). I left the port of Sitka on May 1st and returned on October 4th. During this already too short an interval, I and my subordinate workers were busy prospecting only forty-nine days. The remaining time was lost traveling to Nuchek, to Kotchek Island and to Resurrection Bay, as well as on the troublesome ascent of the Kenai River and the time-consuming transportation of provisions and equipment by backpacking.

In 1851 I left Sitka on May 8th and returned on October 30th, visiting Nuchek and Pavlov Bay on the way back. Sixty-six working days were available this summer and the other time was again spent, for the most part, transporting supplies and equipment. On both occasions, my detachment numbered twelve men.

Under these difficult conditions, I limited my prospecting to . . . [several valleys, streams and canyons of the Kenai River area]. In almost all of these locations, gold was found, but never in amounts greater than one in 240,000 parts of sand. . . .

However paltry these results of my two-year investigation of the Kenai Mountains, they still remained a sufficient justification for the organization of a search for more valuable gold deposits. (In early 1852 I wrote the following from Sitka to Mr. G. A. Josse: "The paucity of these results has cooled the passion of the colonial manager for gold prospecting; activities are suspended. . . . I hear but have no hope that later another engineer with more resources [at his disposal] will have better luck on a path that is now marked. . . .") After excluding the valley of . . . [one river] where, due to a forest fire, I could not have concluded my prospecting systematically, only two valleys and their tributary watercourses were investigated—a very small region in comparison with the surface area throughout the mountains traversing the Kenai Peninsula, and especially when compared also with those coastal mountains of which the Kenais are only one branch. Thus, the exploration for gold and the trifling measure of success with which I had to be satisfied was no more than a small beginning of a project which could take decades to complete in our American colonies. Admittedly, it could also happen that a company of gold-seekers might uncover a rich deposit immediately, with their first test-hole.

(On November 30, 1855, I wrote the following in a letter to General G. P. Helmerson: "I spent the last summer visiting the mountains of the Kenai Peninsula where, at the mouth of the Kenai River I had already found traces of gold in . . . [1848]. This year I persuaded myself that the sandy alluvium at Fort Nicholas [Kenai] . . . is an indication of gold-bearing rock. Even if one finds placer gold only a single time in such alluvial deposits, there is the certain existence also of fragments and debris of gold-bearing veins. This conclusion, as well as the noteworthy discovery of shist or shale with diorite at the source of the Kenai River, caused me to prospect in the upper valley. We obtained color immediately in the first places we tried, and the more we climbed into the valley the more we perceived clearly that still larger flakes were always evident the farther we hiked from our starting place.")

To determine the extent of gold in a given area is the business of science, but one always has Lady Luck to thank for the discovery of rich placers. The probability of an important strike increases, of course, with the size of the area that is prospected thoroughly, but this is, in its turn, determined by the mobility and the number of prospectors; both of the latter conditions were unfavorable during my visits to the colonies.

12

Congressional Debate in 1868

*There is also another letter to the Secretary . . . from
another man that tells a wonderful story. . . . He says he
has discovered a stream of pure verdigris.*

The Russians sold Alaska to the United States in 1867, for
$7,200,000, despite what they knew about its natural wealth.
They had pressing diplomatic problems in Asia and Europe, and Alaska
had become a logistic burden. The United States bought the country
mainly because Secretary of State William Seward (an unreformed
manifest-destinarian of pre-Civil War days) appreciated its geopolitical
uses and resource potential. Most Americans, judging from the
newspapers, favored the purchase—textbook talk about "Seward's
Folly" and the like notwithstanding. The transaction occurred when
Andrew Johnson's political foes were moving to impeach the president.
The purchase treaty was signed quickly and the ceremonial annexation
was performed without delay, then debate over the appropriation
stalled in the House of Representatives. A few clever congressmen
sought to embarrass the Johnson Administration with sly objections to
the purchase, but the outcome of the debate was never really in doubt.

Dramatis Personae
(In Order of Appearance)

Thomas Williams was a Pennsylvania congressman who served as
one of the managers appointed by the House in 1868 to direct the
impeachment proceedings against President Johnson. His concern
about the agricultural possibilities of Alaska might have been more
than political. Although industrialization in the United States was
accelerating at this time, the nation was still mainly agrarian in
thought and employment.

Nathaniel P. Banks, a Republican congressman, was an ardent
proponent of the purchase. He had been governor of Massachusetts and

71

a major general in the Union Army during the Civil War. His habit of falling back without his supplies earned him the name "Commissary Banks" among troops of Confederate General Stonewall Jackson's command.

Cadwallader Colden Washburn, Bank's vocal opponent in the debates, was a representative from Wisconsin and formerly a surveyor and lawyer. He was also a major general in the war just concluded.

Colonel Charles Bulkley directed the Western Union Telegraph Expeditions in the Northwest and Siberia, prior to the transfer of Alaska. His knowledge of Russian America was chiefly second-hand, from employees who had been on the ground. The Telegraph explorers did not visit Cook Inlet.

Henry W. Halleck, still another model major general, commanded the Army in the West when the purchase of Alaska was arranged.

George Davidson was a surveyor and geodesist with the United States Coast Survey. He led a small corps of scientists aboard the Revenue Service (Coast Guard) cutter *Lincoln*, sent by Secretary Seward to gather as much information about Alaska as possible, as fast as possible, between the purchase treaty and the appropriation, to convince members of the House that Russian America was worth the price.

M. D. Teben'kov was a navigator, cartographer and eighth manager of the Russian American Company (1844-1850). He was alive when the congressional debates were underway, but more than likely, he could not have cared less.

W. T. Ballou, an entrepreneur and office-seeker.

Captain W. A. Howard, of the Revenue Service (Coast Guard), commanded the cutter *Lincoln*, sent by the Johnson Administration to reconnoiter Alaska. He decided to visit a few island settlements only. The *Lincoln* did not enter Cook Inlet.

James G. Blaine was a minor figure in this story who later became a major figure in American history. As Secretary of State, he was involved in (among other things) the Bering Sea Controversy over pelagic sealing in the North Pacific. He also ran unsuccessfully for president against Grover Cleveland in 1884. In 1868 he was a congressman from Maine.

P. N. Golovin was a Russian naval captain of the second rank who inspected and reported on the condition of affairs in Alaska during the early 1860's.

John G. Peters was a representative from Maine.

Baron Munchausen was an adventurous character whose tall tales were recounted by R. E. Raspe. He visited Kamchatka but probably not Alaska; however, a recent writer has seen Munchausen's spirit alive in some of the Alaskan stories attributed to Ivan Petroff.

*M*r. WILLIAMS, of Pennsylvania .... in view of the meteorological table embodied in the report of the gentleman from Massachusetts himself, showing that during the summer months it rains about twenty-three days in every month, I ask is not that condition of things entirely at war with the idea of any agricultural capabilities, and this by the law of nature?

Mr. BANKS. The testimony of our own citizens who have gone to the territory since the purchase is conclusive and irresistable in regard to its agricultural capabilities.

Mr. WASHBURN, of Wisconsin. Mr. Chairman, I shall come to that directly. I agree with the gentleman from Massachusetts, that the testimony of the persons who have visited that coast since the purchase is irresistible in regard to agricultural capabilities, and fully sustains what I have said. The gentleman from Massachusetts stood up here and stated to the House that according to the best authority there were twelve million acres of arable land in Alaska. Now I ask the gentleman whether Colonel Bulkley is good authority?

Mr. BANKS. He is good authority.

Mr. WASHBURN, of Wisconsin. I will refer to his testimony in a moment. The southern boundary of Alaska is 54°40'. From that point north to Mount St. Elias, a distance of three hundred miles, Russia owned a strip of land only thirty miles wide. On the whole of this narrow strip there are not a hundred acres of arable land. Sir

George Simpson states that in passing from the southern border up to Sitka he could not find in the whole distance level ground enough for the establishment of a fort. So it is until you get up to Mount St. Elias, which is in latitude 60° or a little more. Now, sir, Colonel Bulkley, who my friend from Massachusetts says is good authority, says: "North of Bristol bay all hopes of successful agriculture must be abandoned. The soil only thaws to the depth of about nine inches, below which we have dug twenty feet through the ice of ages without finding its limit."

Nearly all of Alaska is north of the latitude of Bristol bay, except the peninsula, which is known to be composed of rocks or almost inaccessible mountains. According to this report, which the gentleman from Massachusetts says is a truthful one, there is no agricultural land north of Bristol bay, and if you look at the map you will see that there is very little land south of Bristol bay, agricultural or otherwise. . . .

Well, the treaty was ratified. The next piece of machinery was another telegram from General Halleck; and this bears upon the agricultural question. Two days before we met last November General Halleck sends a telegram on here stating that it is very necessary to have the land surveyed upon the peninsula of Kenay, as agricultural settlers would be going there. Of course, this dispatch was not intended to have any effect upon Congress, which was to meet two days thereafter. But the importance of having these lands surveyed at once and in mid-winter, in latitude 65°, in the interests of agriculture, could not be overlooked or the information wait the slow progress of the mails. For the benefit of the agriculturists who are invited to Cook's inlet and Prince William's sound by the general commanding on the Pacific coast, I will set before them the entertainment to which they are invited. I quote from the report of Professor Davidson:

> Tebenkoff (1848) gives a dark picture of the appearance and climate of Prince William's sound, calling it desolate, gloomy, and deserted; surrounded by rocks and pine forests, mountains covered with eternal snow, and enveloped in perpetual fog or invisible with drizzling rain. Rain falls sometimes for a whole month; and there are not more than sixty or ninety sunny days in the year. During the months of July and August the thermometer showed 59° on fair days and 46° on rainy days. The

frost in winter is very severe, but of short duration, for the south winds change it suddenly to thaw and rain.

The peninsula of Kenay is between Cook's inlet and Prince William's sound, and is the land which General Halleck wants to have surveyed in the interest of agriculture; and they all concede that this land thus described by Tebenkoff is the best land they have in the territory.

* * *

Mr. BANKS. As the gentleman from Wisconsin refers to the testimony of Professor Davidson, I will ask to have an extract of a letter from him read.

Mr. WASHBURN, of Wisconsin. Give me the page, and I will find it.

Mr. BANKS. I will send it to the Clerk's desk to be read.

Mr. WASHBURN, of Wisconsin. I object to that letter being read. Anything Professor Davidson has reported officially I do not object to having read. But I am opposed to the reading of any of this manufactured testimony recently got up for the purpose of getting through the treaty.

Mr. BANKS. The gentleman asked for testimony as to coal in Alaska, and I have given it. . . .

Mr. BANKS. I hope the gentleman from Wisconsin will allow Mr. Davidson's letter to be read.

Mr. WASHBURN, of Wisconsin. Well, as my friend from Massachusetts has shown anxiety to have the extract of the letter of Professor Davidson read, I will yield for that purpose. It is so seldom he produces any authority I like to oblige him, though his authority should prove nothing.

The Clerk read as follows:

> At Coal Harbor, on Unga Island, Graham harbor in Cook's inlet, and one locality in Chatham strait, the company had opened veins of lignite for fuel for their steamers, but the results were unfavorable and operations abandoned. At . . . [Kachemak] bay, in Cook's inlet, there is a seven-feet seam of true coal, but it has not been worked, as I understand. It crops out at or near low water, and would require greater expense and more engineering talent than the company commanded. This out-crop exhibits itself at intervals for twenty miles along the shore toward the northwest. My party discovered water worn pieces of coal

much intermixed with foreign substances for four or five miles along the head of a stream, coming through a heavy forest, and opening upon a fine bay. An examination of the specimens proves it bituminous, but the bed or beds from which it is broken will, when discovered, afford coal of vastly superior quality to any heretofore known to exist on the Pacific coast. Coal for steamship purposes is the great desideratum of the Pacific. With a supply of good coal within the distance of Sitka from San Francisco, California, Oregon and Washington will at once be relieved from the necessity of freighting their coal from fourteen thousand five hundred to seventeen thousand five hundred miles, at a cost to the consumer of twenty dollars per ton in gold. Appreciating this great drawback, and impressed by the analysis of the specimens we obtained and all the favorable geological indications, I have urged the importance of a special and exhaustive exploration of the locality.

Mr. WASHBURN, of Wisconsin. Mr. Chairman, I have listened to the reading of that letter, and I hesitate not to assert that there is no proof contained therein that there is a vein of coal any where in Alaska. Mr. Davidson does not pretend that he ever saw a vein of coal there. He says in his report, speaking on that subject, that he is informed there is coal there. He says in his letter, just read, that coal is worth twenty dollars a ton in gold. Is it possible that a seven-foot vein of coal exists on Cook's inlet, and not opened while coal is worth twenty dollars a ton? The statement is preposterous. It is on a par with another letter that I have here by a Mr. Ballou, which I will read. One W. T. Ballou, of San Francisco, wrote the Secretary as follows:

San Francisco, September 7, 1867

My Dear Sir: Since my last with inclosures a vessel arrived in this port from Kodiak. The following is a copy of a letter received by me:

"Mr. Ballou: We beg to inform you that we have at last found the seam of coal that we have hunted so long—no thanks to the R. A. Co. It is wonderful, over thirty feet deep, pure anthracite; we trace it one mile; good harbor; oak and fir timber. Our fortune is made; thanks to you alone. We hope to see you soon.

A. & G. MARSH"

The above is *verbatim*. This is only one instance of the great mineral resources of that country. I know of others more astonishing, and had I funds sufficient, quickly would I develop astonishing facts that would soon make Alaska in many respects vie with almost any portion of our country; but, as I said in my first letter to you, it is no agricultural country. Its minerals, fish, and furs are enough.

Should I not be honored by a Government position, as applied for in my last, and some of your eastern capitalists want to form a company whose capital shall be $100,000 or more, I will take $10,000 of stock and manage the affair so as to double the money in two years or I'll lose my head. To do this will require immediate attention and no delay, as the ground must be occupied before the immigration flocks in. My reference can be had and money at any time required. As I suppose I am wearying your patience I close till some reply.

Yours,   W. T. BALLOU

Hon. William H. Seward, Secretary of State

It will be seen hereafter that Captain Howard, of the revenue service, was at Kodiak after this pretended coal discovery, and though constantly looking out for coal, failed either to discover or hear of any on that island.

There is also another letter to the Secretary in this book from another man and tells a wonderful story, almost equal to that of the gentleman from Idaho. He says he has discovered a stream of pure verdigris in Alaska.

Mr. Chairman, I have been furnished by a gallant gentleman, (a native of that country which has been absorbed by Russia; a gentleman who served gallantly and faithfully in our Army, and whom it was my pleasure to know during the war, while he was serving on the staff on one of our most accomplished commanders,) with a translation of some Russian documents on this subject.

Before, however, alluding to them, I wish to call attention to the concluding passage of Captain Howard's report, as I find that my time will compel me to dismiss him without further notice. This modern Jason, who was sent up to Alaska in pursuit of the golden fleece—

Mr. BLAINE. And came back shorn.

Mr. WASHBURN, of Wisconsin. Yes, and came back shorn, if we may judge by the conclusion of his report, which is as follows:

On the 18th of November Captain Howard arrived in San Francisco. He says:

"Thus ended the observatory cruise of the *Lincoln*. Regretting that so little has been effected, by the lateness of the season and the extremely boisterous and rainy weather," ... "I beg leave, however, to bear testimony to the untiring exertions of Mr. Davidson and Coast Survey party to accomplish an almost impossibility. For many days and nights they watched in vain for sun, moon, and stars, which led us almost to believe that neither ever had been or would be seen."

I will now refer to the translation of the Russian document, being a description of that country. Captain Golowin, of the Russian navy, was sent out in 1860 and 1861, and made a report to the high admiral, Duke Constantine. I will read a passage for the satisfaction of my friend who has seen a man who saw a tree in Alaska three feet in diameter, that was prone upon the ground inclosed by the roots of another tree of the same size, and yet the first tree was as sound as when growing in the forest.

Mr. PETERS. Was the man who saw the tree named Munchausen?

Mr. WASHBURN, of Wisconsin. I have forgotten his name. It sounded to me something like that. But I think Baron Munchausen never got off anything so good as that. . . .

13

The
Army Arrives
1868 - 1869

by Alfred L. Hough

. . . [Ninilchik] looked peacable and home like with its
cottages, outhouses, stacks of hay, and cattle grazing
on the plain. I wished I could land and talk with
these Arcadians.

The establishment of American authority over the region did not begin auspiciously. Cook Inlet won the first round. The ship *Torrent*, carrying Battery "F" of the Second U.S. Army Artillery to Kenai, was wrecked near Dangerous Cape on the southeast coast of the Inlet during the summer of 1868. The troops survived to occupy new Fort Kenai the following year, and to entertain there an inspection by Major General George H. Thomas of the Army's Division of the Pacific. His aide de camp, Captain Hough, described the countryside and population in 1869.

*J*uly 31st. The climate of this country is an anomaly to me, we arose to find a beautiful summer morning, our heavy clothing rather uncomfortable. Went ashore and walked up to the Post by a walk lined with green grasses of many kinds, sprinkled with a variety of wild flowers like an Illinois prairie in spring. The Post is the old Russian trading Post of St. Nicholas, established 102 years ago. The buildings are a cluster of log houses, dark and close, among them a little Greek Church. The ground, originally covered with timber is cleared for some distance and promising gardens occupied part of it. Shade trees planted near the houses were bright and green, and the whole place looked really pretty. It being the Russian American Sabbath (Saturday) we went to the Church. It is a miniature copy of the one at Sitka, the congregation all Indians, the Priest a half breed, and it is said a drunkard, like the rest. The Indians from the small village near all attend the church regularly.

There is only one Russian family here, its head being a trader, he is also a Church officer.

We lunched with the officers who gave us the best they had, pork, beans, tea, bread, butter and canned fruits; they had but little furniture, but with it a piano bought of a Russian resident. There are no ladies in the garrison, but at the suttlers I saw some hooped skirts, these I suppose are for the laundresses for certainly the squaws don't use them, in fact don't wear much of anything at this season. After spending a pleasant morning it unfortunately began to rain again, and we had to return to the ship. From all I can learn this plateau and a corresponding region in . . . [Bristol Bay on Bering Sea], have the most favorable climate in Alaska. They have good summers from April to August with but little rain, but the winters are severe. The small amount of rain is accounted for by the distance from the mountains. This was exemplified today, for though it was bright and clear here, we could not see the mountains in the distance for the fogs and clouds.

Just before going to the vessel the General had a "big talk" with two Indian Chiefs, one of the band here, the other of one some 80 miles north who happened here on a trading visit. The talk was long and conducted through two interpreters, an Indian who spoke Indian and Russian, and Capt Archimendatioff who spoke Russian and English. One of the Chiefs was quite eloquent, and both upon hearing a speech of the Generals that the great Chief at Washington intended the troops to protect them from bad white men, and to help them to improve their condition, took off their hats and bowed low to him with thanks. One said this day was like a grand holiday, as no American Chief had talked to them so kind before.

We met a curious character here, a Prussian named "Bischoff" a littled dried up old man who had spent 40 years of his life in the wilds of America collecting insects, birds &c for scientific institutions. He is now working for the Smithsonian Institute. He barely makes a living and works for the love of his Science. He is known here as the "bug catcher" and until the General, who knew of him, came to his relief by going security for supplies for him, had been living for some time on charity from the Post, and the Indians, his remittances having failed him.

The officers and men here are more cheerful and happy looking than at any other Post I have seen in Alaska. I attribute this to the brighter climate they have here. I fear however they will not be so happy looking by next spring after six months of night and eight of snow and rain. We are just too late for the salmon fishing which I regret, as the salmon here are the largest on the coast. The troops have laid in a winter's supply, the average weight of the catch was 40# each, the heaviest one weighed 75#. I saw them in casks cut up like mess pork and packed like it. At dinner we celebrated the Generals 54th birthday, and had a pleasant time, but the night set in with steady rain. We have Alaskan weather at all the Posts while we are at them for a certainty.

August 1st. Raining again today, but we went ashore. I spent most of the time in the traders store witnessing the trading with the Indians. A band from the North had some furs to trade, and it was amusing to watch them. They would only trade for silver half dollars, and then would immediately spend all the money. They all talked at once, though the business of each man was done by himself, and all through an interpreter. There was much haggling about the prices and the Indians would sell only one article at a time (a trait I have since found all Indians to have). I was present at a very interesting time, the change from the Russian measure to the American, which was accomplished today. The Russian measure, with an unpronouncable [*sic*] name, is about 3/4 of a yard. This had been used heretofore.

The Indians had observed that the soldiers bought with our measure, and had demanded for some time that they should have the same. This was granted them today, and the prices per measure raised accordingly. This astounded them; they insisted upon getting the yard for the same money as they had been giving for the Russian measure. There was a great pow-wow about this but after some explanation appeared to be satisfied and began dealing. When it was found they had raised the prices of their furs though they were paid for them in half dollars, here was another stoppage, and after more speeches, and some apparently elaborate orations to the young men from their Chief, they reduced their prices to the old standard, and all went on again apparently satisfied.

* * *

On the morning of the 2nd of August after having a salmon caught for us close by the ship weighing 65# we got under way, and bid good bye to Kenay bound for Kodiac. Our list of passengers increased one by a young black bear, we had a pleasant sail down the inlet, renewed our acquaintance with the snow mountains and glaciers, and passed near enough to [Ninilchik] to have a good view. It looked peacable [*sic*] and home like with its cottages, outhouses, stacks of hay, and cattle grazing on the plain. I wished I could land and talk with these Arcadians. Late in the afternoon we turned into . . . [Kachemak] Bay on the east coast, run up it 15 miles and anchored. Our object here was to get some samples of coal which was done, and we were off again before midnight. Next morning found us at sea in the open Pacific, and without incident—except speaking the little schooner "Margaret" from Kodiac to Kenay with Government supplies, and shooting at whales from on deck.

14

A White-Water Adventure in 1870

by Polaris

. . . [The Indians] trap only one of the seven [beaver] lakes each year, thus leaving ample time for repletion of the stock in the interval, and I would not advise any white trappers to interfere with this prudent arrangement.

Fort Kenai's "brighter climate" and a plentiful supply of fat salmon did not induce the Army to linger long. There was little need for a military force. The natives were quiescent, the non-natives were few in number, and commercial activity was limited to the old fur trade. In 1868 small trading posts were established at Knik, Kenai and English Bay. The trade—indeed, inland travel generally—often required laborious cordelling and paddling upstream, and exciting descents of Alaska's swift rivers.

One white-water journey was described by a correspondent for the *San Francisco Chronicle*, writing under the name "Polaris." The trip (he said) was inspired by the beaver trade and rumors of Doroshin's successful gold prospecting twenty years earlier. The following account concludes with Polaris' failure to find any gold. He then visited with "the Chief from Skilak" and traveled to a chain of nearby beaver lakes. The Indians, he noted, "trap only one of the seven lakes each year, thus leaving ample time for repletion of the stock in the interval, and I would not advise any white trappers to interfere with this prudent arrangement." After sampling a tasty piece of broiled beaver, he allowed, "what with eating beaver, sleeping on beaver, and covering myself with beaver, it was not to be wondered at that I dreamed all night I was gnawing off a huge tree, and awoke in the morning with a toothache." Such abundance quickly vanished as later white trappers failed to heed the wise counsel of Polaris. (His identity is revealed in note #14.)

While I was at the old trading post of . . . [Kenai], on Cook's Inlet, in the Summer of 1870, reports reached me, through different channels, of an expedition in search of gold which had been undertaken some twenty years ago by a Russian mining official with a number of soldiers; even the amount of gold found by this man was given—eighty-four ounces—but for some reason the enterprise stopped there and was never resumed. As soon as opportunity served, I concluded to follow up the trail of this gold-seeker, said to have been successful, and find out for myself what foundation there was for this report. Business with some of the beaver-trappers called me up into the mountains, and as the region which tempted my curiosity lay in the same direction, I managed to combine both objects.

The first part of my route led up the Kenai River, past Tlough Willan, and I secured the services of Stepanka, the trusty companion of former trips, and his younger brother, Ravrousha, a stout lad of 16. Our whole equipment consisted of a covered skin canoe (bidarka), our rifles, bear knives and ammunition, for the journey before us would lead us over some rough country, and we intended to travel unemcumbered and live, like Sherman, on what we could pick up along the line of march. By carrying the canoe by the rapids and over the trail along Tlough Willan Canyon we reached the old camping-place in two days. A ten-pound trout and a brace of grouse served as a tolerable excuse for a more dainty supper, and the old store-house at the place offered us better shelter than we could expect to find during the remainder of the trip.

Early the next morning we launched the canoe, as a stretch of comparatively smooth water lay before us, and having very little more than our own weight to propel, we made good time. Like everywhere else in Alaska the timber increased in size with the distance from the sea-shore. To the birch, spruce and alder was added cottonwood of very respectable proportions, and as the bluffs rose higher and higher on the banks of the river, even yellow pine appeared. There was such beauty of scenery as I had never expected to see under that latitude, judging from the stunted vegetation on the coast. Here huge trees hang over the majestic stream. The snow-white trunks of the birch gleaming forth from between the thick underbrush, while the soil is covered with a bright green carpet of moss, variegated by a pretty pattern of clustering red cranberries and golden thimbleberries. The deep-blue sky overhead and the genial sun in the heavens from 2 o'clock in the morning until about 11 at night make life under the "arctic circle" more tolerable than people imagine at that time of the year.

But there is a drawback to every enjoyment here below. Here it is the ubiquitous mosquito, and such an industrious, powerful, exasperating variety of this never very loveable insect as it has never been my misfortune to meet anywhere else. Toward the close of that day the channel of the river became very much impeded by rocks, and at many places where we had to exert all our strength at the paddle, and all our attention was required to watch the slightest deviation of the prow of our frail craft from her course, we were left at the mercy of our fierce little winged assailants, unable to ward them off except by spasmodic twitch-winking of eyelids—both very primitive and unsatisfactory means of defense. As we approached the big lake of . . . [Skilak], out of which flows the Kenai, the evil was even increased ten-fold by the enrollment under the mosquito banner of myriads of small black flies, which left a mark after every bite, red as blood and of the size of a pea.

Stepanka, who was steering, now told us that we would have some hard paddling to do before we could reach the lake and camp. These bidarkas are skittish things to navigate in; only a slight willow frame about a foot deep, fifteen in length, round-bottomed and covered with the tanned seal skin all over, with the exception of three round holes on top for the men to get in. They are easily capsized even when laden or ballasted, but ours was empty and light as a feather, so that I was actually afraid to think on one side of my head for fear of upsetting.

At last the lake was in sight, a noble sheet of water, forty miles in length and from five to twenty broad, and I was already anticipating the luxury of a savory supper and, above all, a good "scratch," when our steersman's voice warned me to attend to my paddle. A ledge of rocks was stretching from one shore almost to the middle of the channel, and by its outward point the water rushed furiously. Slowly we paddled up to the point through the smooth water formed by the ledge, and then, throwing our whole strength on our paddles on our port side, tried to shoot past the obstacle; but the current caught our projecting bow and swept us around, down stream, making us lose in a few seconds the work of half an hour. Again we tried it, and once again, with no better luck. I spoke about landing and making a portage, but Stepanka scorned to give up the battle, and then I saw him perform a feat which many a professional gymnast would fail to imitate. He made us paddle up to the dreaded ledge once more until our prow almost touched the rock, just outside of the reach of the foaming waters of the current; then he shouted: "Golovah doloi!" (down with your heads!) and when I in the middle hole stooped down, he rose to his feet and jumped over me on to the "deck" (if one might call it thus) without even stirring the feather-like structure, which a touch of the hand on one side would upset. Shouting to his brother to stoop down, he jumped over him and then on to the outer edge of the rock, at the same time catching hold of the bow of the canoe and drawing it past the rock until he could step into his own place again, and with a few good strokes of the paddles we shot into the smooth waters of the lake and soon were camped in a sheltered grove on its banks.

Ravrousha speared some fish and gathered berries, but that night I could not eat. During the latter part of the day's journey I had removed my moccasins and rolled up my sleeves in order to be ready for a swim, and the flies and mosquitos, with the meanness characteristic of their kind, had feasted undisturbed on the portions of my cuticle thus trustingly exposed. When I left the canoe I had calves which would have drawn a prize at an exhibition of pet footmen in London, and arms, neck and face corresponded in size. A burning fever raged in my veins, and I tossed in agony for the greater part of the night. So much for Alaska mosquitos. Their time is short, only two months out of twelve, but they make the most of it.

The following morning I felt better, and as we expected to get to the spot where the Russian officer prospected that night, I concluded to go on. Stepanka promised us a good breakfast on one of the many islands in the lake, and we embarked at once. A short pull over the placid waters of the lake brought us to a low, sandy island, with a pyramidical rock in the center. Birds of various kinds were roosting in the sand, and some "candle-fish," a kind of smelt fat enough to cook in its own grease, fried with duck eggs, proved a very acceptable meal after my compulsory fast of the night before. From here the journey over the lake was pleasant; only once we had to seek shelter from a sudden squall, which lashed the water into respectable waves in no time, but it subsided as suddenly as it arose.

High, snow-capped peaks surrounded the lake on all sides but that where the Kenai forms an outlet to this huge body of water. Fish in great variety abound, and all sorts of aquatic fowl can be killed with sticks on the nest, so little alarmed are they at the approach of man. Toward evening we approached the mouth of one of the many mountain torrents, when within fifty yards of us, a group of reindeer came to the beach to drink. They were large, with broad, heavy antlers, and while gracefully sipping the sparkling liquid, looking trustingly around with their great blue eyes, formed too pretty a picture to be disturbed. But Ravrousha had no such scruples; his rifle cracked, and the little family bounded away, leaving one member stretched on the sand.

When we landed Stepanka showed me a spot where traces of an encampment of Europeans were still visible. There had been a breastwork and log houses; of the latter only the foundations were left, but some little pieces of broken shovels and other tools gave me the assurance that there was some foundation to the story of the gold-seeker of twenty years ago, and dreams and visions of gold haunted my couch that night. In the morning we went about a mile up the bed of the mountain stream, and there was convincing evidence of some extensive prospecting in former times. A shaft had been sunk to the depth of about eighty feet, ten feet of it being filled with water. By the help of a rope of strips of deer-skin the two Indians lowered me some forty feet into the shaft, where a drift had been started; I crawled into it but it extended only a few yards into the side of the shaft and, taking some gravel from different parts of the shaft and drift in my hankerchief I returned to daylight once more. During the afternoon I panned out the gravel, but, owing, perhaps, to my want of experience, I failed to discover the slightest trace of the precious metal, and in the evening we started again on our journey, leaving the problem of the existence of gold still unsolved. . . .

15

Eldorado in 1883

by J. A. Jacobsen

Certainly the brown bears appeared not to have very much fear of us, for at one place we saw two huge specimens on an encircling, snow-patched, rocky slope, rolling around like balls and playing with each other like kittens. . . .

Shortly after . . . [the Russians] built Fort Kenai, they sailed one day in many boats to Soonroodna and abducted from here—in a second edition of the rape of the Sabine women—all of the young girls and women. . . .

During the first two decades of American rule, the human, plant, and animal life of Cook Inlet changed but little. A few trading vessels sailed into the bay, a few mineral investigators came and went, and a few fishermen tested the Inlet's piscatorial potential. The period has been called by some historians an "era of neglect"; the label comes in part from an overweening faith in the wisdom of economic development, a pernicious definition of progress, and an apparent dislike of the land and its natural wonders.

One foreign visitor, in 1883, reacted more sympathetically toward the wild landscape. Captain J. Adrian Jacobsen was a Scandinavian engaged in the collection of Alaskan anthropological evidence for the Berlin Museum für Völkerkunde. To reach the Inlet, he came overland from Bristol Bay via the old portage past Iliamna Lake to Kamishak Bay. What he found he praised in the florid rhetoric of his more poetic age.

*T*he shoreline scenery is delightfully beautiful. The mountains are crowned with high, pointed summits and are approached with difficulty from the sea. From here we can observe in the far distance the smoke from the lofty volcano Iliamna. Snow, which covers all of the highest parts of the mountains, merges at the lower elevations with different glaciers, and the coast itself is enveloped in fresh greenery. A splendid fragrance fills the air near the birches along the shore. The craggy beach was, through the combined action of rain and rivulet as well as sea-wave, broken and cleft and remains a picturesque sight, with its caves, pillars, arches and gullies.

As we passed . . . [Chinitna] Bay, three times we saw where smoke was rising below the top of Iliamna, and the snow below the crater was of dirty gray color, as if sooty water had been poured over it. To prepare our tea, we sailed into the estuary of one of the many rivers that flow into this bay. In doing so we noticed almost everywhere the tracks of brown bears; we also repeatedly caught sight of these animals if we stirred around near the beach. Certainly the brown bears appeared not to have very much fear of us, for at one place we saw two huge specimens on an encircling, snow-patched, rocky slope, rolling around like balls and playing with each other like kittens; at another place Master Brown remained for a time standing quietly and contemplating our expedition, until finally he took flight through the bushes.

This region is truly an Eldorado for hunters and tourists. The exciting landscape—volcanic eruptions, glaciers, romantic rock formations, waterfalls, grottoes and caves—joins together with a wealth of animals such as I have seldom seen. The rivers teem with salmon and other fishes, the bay offers the pleasures of the seal-hunt; bear, moose and caribou are met with in abundance. The cliffs in many locations are blanketed with millions of sea gull nests, on which now—as we pass along—brooding mothers sit while their mates slice the air in dashing flight and raise such an alarm that we can scarcely be understood among ourselves.

* * *

[Jacobsen stopped at Tuxedni Bay, Tyonek, Kenai, Kasilof, Ninilchik, Anchor Point, Seldovia Bay and English Bay; at the latter place he learned that a schooner operated by a Captain Sand[s] and a Mr. Frank was scheduled to return to Kodiak in two weeks.]

On the day of my arrival, Mr. Frank imparted the information that farther up Kachemak Bay from where I crossed are situated the ruins of an old, abandoned native village named Soonroodna, and that it would possibly repay the effort to make an excavation at this home of the Hardak (also called the Hardanak) Eskimos. Because I still had more than a week to wait for the departure of the schooner, I resolved to utilize the time for such an excavation, although it meant traveling again, this time backtracking a distance of about thirty English miles. I left Fort Alexander [English Bay] on June 26, after I had hired some helpers for a very dear price, and on the afternoon of the same day I arrived again at . . . Seldovia Bay, where I engaged as a guide an old Indian whose forefathers had lived in the abandoned village. We traveled still farther on the same day, to little Yukon Island, where we collected our first eggs and shot our first bird, and where we stayed overnight in a house owned by the old Indian. My host sold me some old stone lamps and a pair of dance-rattles.

In the morning we sailed closely around Yukon Island and shot, along its shore, ten sea-parrots, auks and other birds, as well as a large spotted seal; the bag will prove a very useful addition to our slightly depleted reserve supplies. After some hours of speedier sailing, we finally arrived in the strange other world of the ruined town. The place is located below the three glaciers on the south coast of Kachemak Bay.

Soonroodna was a large village even before . . . [the early 1790's], when the Russians came. Shortly after they had built Fort Kenai, they sailed one day in many boats to Soonroodna and abducted from here—in a second edition of the rape of the Sabine women—all of the young girls and women, whom they took to the Fort and in this way procured wives. The natives, who saw that they were powerless against the Russians, abandoned their home in angry sorrow and scattered themselves around Kodiak Island, to settle there anew among the Eskimo inhabitants.

Before the advent of the Russians, the original inhabitants of Soonroodna cremated their dead and buried the remains. They were all that was left when the residents themselves abandoned the village. Old dance masks were preserved in a grotto to serve the dead and remained intact as awesome religious objects to the descendants. Anyone who visited the isolated spot would be obliged to offer as a sacrifice to these masks and the spirit of the dead, some object, usually food, and also a nice little basket with an excellent pattern [of weaving], in which the inhabitants of the earlier period (and those today also) could bring water to a boil with the help of heated stones. My old Indian guide claimed to know a place where the ancient natives deposited their dead and funereal objects. It was this cave that we sought. But with the passage of time, the rocky cliff above had collapsed, crushing and shattering all artifacts (as we could plainly see). Any effort on our part to move these enormous boulders was in vain; I was able to pull out only a few little fragments.

16

A Great Eruption in 1883

by George Davidson

*At night, from a distance of fifty or sixty miles, flames
can be seen issuing from the summit of the volcano;
and in the day-time vast volumes of smoke roll from it.*

Captain Jacobsen eventually had better luck; he returned to
English Bay with a number of artifacts. On July 7, he left the
Inlet for Kodiak. If he had remained for three months to pursue his
elusive archaeological treasures, he would have witnessed one of those
awesome natural catastrophes that occasionally dramatize the
restlessness of Alaska's landscape. In October Augustine Volcano
erupted violently. George Davidson of the U.S. Coast and Geodetic
Survey, from second-hand reports, described the event for *Science*
magazine. A later note by William Healey Dall modified the Davidson
report: "According to the correspondent of the [San Francisco]

Bulletin, the account of the eruption of the volcano on Augustine Island, Cook's Inlet, sent by the last advices of 1883, was much exaggerated. The island 'was not split in two, and no new island was formed; but the west side of the summit has fallen in, forming a new crater, while the whole island has risen to such an extent as to fill up the only bay or boat harbor, and to extend the reefs, or sea-otter rocks, running out from the island in various directions.' The hunting-party feared to be lost has arrived safely in Kodiak. No tidal waves were observed on the west shore of Cook's Inlet or on Kodiak Island." Nevertheless, the eruption must have been spectacular.

About eight o'clock on the morning of Oct. 6, 1883, the weather being beautifully clear, the wind light from the south-westward . . . , and the tide at dead low water, the settlers and fishing-parties at English Harbor heard a heavy report to windward (Augustin bearing south-west by west three-fourths west by compass). So clear was the atmosphere that the opposite or north-western coast of the inlet was in clear view at a distance of more than sixty miles.

When the heavy explosion was heard, vast and dense volumes of smoke were seen rolling out of the summit of St. Augustin, and moving to the north-eastward (or up the inlet) under the influence of the lower stratum of wind; and, at the same time (according to the statements of a hunting-party of natives in Kamishak Bay), a column of white vapor arose from the sea near the island, slowly ascending, and gradually blending with the clouds. The sea was also greatly agitated and boiling, making it impossible for boats to land upon or to leave the island.

From English Harbor (Port Graham) it was noticed that the columns of smoke, as they gradually rose, spread over the visible heavens, and obscured the sky, doubtless under the influence of a higher current. . . . Fine pumice-dust soon began to fall, but gently, some of it being very fine, and some very soft, without grit.

At about twenty-five minutes past eight A.M., or twenty-five minutes after the great eruption, a great "earthquake wave," estimated as from twenty-five to thirty feet high, came upon Port

101

Graham like a wall of water. It carried off all the fishing-boats from the point, and deluged the houses. This was followed, at intervals of about five minutes, by two other large waves, estimated at eighteen and fifteen feet; and during the day several large and irregular waves came into the harbor. The first wave took all the boats into the harbor, the receding wave swept them back again to the inlet, and they were finally stranded. Fortunately it was low water, or all of the people at the settlement must inevitably have been lost. The tides rise and fall about fourteen feet. . . .

The condition of the island of Augustin or Chernaboura ["black-brown"], according to the latest accounts, is this:—

At night, from a distance of fifty or sixty miles, flames can be seen issuing from the summit of the volcano; and in the day-time vast volumes of smoke roll from it. Upon nearer approach from English Harbor, it was found that the mountain had been split in two from peak to base by a great rupture extending across it from east to west, and that the northern slope of the mountain had sunk away to the level of the northern cliff. This is corroborated by the statement of the hunting-party in Kamishak Bay. Smoke issued from the peak at a very short distance to the southward of the rupture.

The party of natives on Kamishak did not approach the islet, though they gave clear and distinct accounts of its eruption and subsequent appearance; but Capt. C. T. Sands, who was at English Harbor, gave the Alaska company a full description; and Capt. Cullie of the [schooner] *Kodiak* states, that, if there were plenty of water in the line of rupture, it would be possible for a vessel to sail through. At the time of Capt. Sands' observations the low ground of the island was visible, and seemed to be a vast crater, from which smoke and flames were issuing.

But beyond all these phenomena, apart from the volcanic eruption and the rupture of the island, we have the report of Capt. Cullie . . . , who approached the island from English Harbor on the 10th of November, and found that a new island, about a mile and a half long and seventy-five feet high, had been upheaved in the ten-fathom passage between Augustin and the mainland to the westward. This passage is from six to eight miles wide, and was sailed through by Puget in Vancouver's voyages of discovery.

This new island (also reported by the hunting-party in Kamishak) would appear to have arisen during the late volcanic activity. It lies to the north-westward of Chernaboura Island (Augustin), and was distinctly seen from the *Kodiak*, as that vessel lay ten miles to the north-eastward, and had clear weather.

To show the violence of the volcanic convulsions at this time, two extinct volcanoes on the Alaska peninsula, which are reported to be about west (true) from the active volcano Iliamna (twelve thousand feet high), had burst into activity; and during the day volumes of smoke were distinctly seen, and columns of flame at night. Usually, at that season, Augustin and the peak are covered with deep snow. On the 10th of November, however, when Capt. Cullie approached the island, while there was a depth of four feet of snow at Port Graham (English Harbor), Mount St. Augustin was bare and black.

During the same season, a party of seven or eight Aleuts had established themselves on Chernaboura (Augustin) Island to hunt the otter during the winter. Two of the women refused to remain on account of the violent noises inside Mount St. Augustin; and they were taken to St. Paul, Kodiak. Since the eruption no one of this party has been seen, nor any signs of their bidarkas, although a rescuing party of natives had gone along the coast to learn of their whereabouts. It is feared, therefore, that they have been destroyed. In confirmation of this report of the native women, Capt. Sands says that he and others noticed that St. Augustin was emitting smoke as far back as August; but no other signs were observed before the heavy report of Oct. 6. ◼

17

The Salmon Fishery at the End of the Century

by Claude Cane

... every fish in the trap is killed and carried off to the cannery, where the selection is made, those for which they have no use being simply thrown over the side of the staging into the river to lie there and rot.

The oldest continuous industry of any size in Cook Inlet is fishing. The Inlet, reported J. F. Moser of the Fish Commission Steamer *Albatross* in 1898, "is very difficult ... to fish. There are probably plenty of salmon to supply several canneries, but they are not only difficult to catch, ... the fisheries and the conditions attending the serving of the canneries are extremely hazardous. ... Nearly every season some lives are lost in the swift currents of Cook Inlet." According to Moser, the Alaska Packing Company of San Francisco built a cannery on the right bank of the Kasilof River, at the mouth, in 1882. It was sold to the Arctic Fishing Company in 1885 but did not operate in 1890 when the cannery ship *Corea* was wrecked in the Inlet; in 1893 the Company joined the Alaska Packer's Association. A cannery built in 1888 at Kenai joined the Association in 1893; it had not operated since 1891. George Hume constructed another cannery at Kasilof in 1890, and entered the Association in 1893, after ceasing operations. Since then, fish-processing on the Inlet has frequently undergone such "rationalization."

The one cannery left in 1896 packed just under 400,000 salmon in about 35,000 cases. Thirty-three percent of the king salmon were taken in traps and 67% in gill nets; 87% of the red salmon were taken in traps; nearly all of the silvers were taken in gill nets; and nearly all of the humpies were from traps. The labor force in 1897 consisted of thirty-five white fishermen; eight whites, twenty natives, and 100 Chinese worked in the cannery. The "Chinese contract" was 42½ cents a case. Fishermen received board, $30 a month, and ¾ of a cent per case for their "extremely hazardous" work. Of the latter, said Moser, "A number . . . remain in the country during the winter, and hunt and trap; some are squaw men. The cannery ship remains at anchor in Tuxedni Harbor, under Chisik Island, on the western shore of the inlet, as the anchorage off the cannery is unsafe."

The fishery has had bad years, due to greed, excessive sport fishing on spawning streams, inadequate scientific study of the salmon, poor game management, and the vagaries of the fish itself. Now, many of the Inlet's fishermen believe their renewable resource is threatened by extractive industries, particularly petroleum and timber. They are probably right. But in the summer of 1902, when an Englishman toured the Kasilof cannery, the industry had fish to waste—and did.

*T*he *Jennie* was not to leave ... [Kasilof] till the evening ebb, so we spent the rest of the day with the Wetherbees [the superintendent] and went round the cannery—a most interesting visit to me as I had never been over one before. This cannery, which belongs to the Alaska Packers' Association, is the largest and best equipped on Cook's Inlet, and although there are larger ones which turn out a bigger pack in Alaska, I doubt if there is one better managed. The usual yearly pack from ... [Kasilof] amounts to from 25,000 to 30,000 cases of 48 cans, each containing 1 lb. of salmon. This year was a record year, and totted up to 33,000 cases. It might have been considerably larger, but there were no more cans, the whole supply having been used up.

There are five distinct varieties of salmon, viz., the King salmon, the Alaskan Red, the Silver or Spring salmon, the Humpback or Humpie, and the Dog salmon. The first three are known further south by the names of the Tyhee, Sockeye, and Cohoe. Of these five only the first two are used for canning purposes, unless the run is a very short one, when a few thousand cases may be made up of Silver salmon or Humpies. The Dog salmon is never used, and even the Indians despise him. There seems to be no reason for this except that his flesh is white instead of red. I have eaten many, and like them next best to the King salmon. This latter is a magnificent fish, which runs sometimes up to a weight of 100 lb. in Alaskan waters. I have seen one myself on the scales which pulled down 87 lb., and when I state that in the cannery they reckon that one King, on an average, means one case of salmon or 48 lb., and that in order to be canned he has to be divested of head, tail, fins, and guts, it is evident that the *average* weight of those brought in must be over 50 lb. as they come out of the water. They will take a spoon at the mouths of the rivers, but no one ever thinks of fishing for them with rod and line. They are too plentiful and too easily caught in other ways. The greater part of the pack is made up of Red salmon, which run quite small from 5 lb. to 7 lb., and have flesh of the deep red colour familiar to those who eat canned salmon. In my opinion it is the worst fish of all for the table, being dry and tasteless; but I believe the public likes the colour and will have it.

Considering that it is no uncommon thing for 20,000 salmon to be caught in a single trap in twenty-four hours, and that a large proportion of those are of the other three varieties and therefore thrown away as useless, it is evident that the waste of fish life attendant on every cannery is enormous. The rejected fish are not let loose to swim away, but every fish in the trap is killed and carried off to the cannery, where the selection is made, those for which they have no use being simply thrown over the side of the staging into the river to lie there and rot. One would imagine that it would pay the various canning companies to establish factories for the manufacture of fish oil and manure from these wasted fish, and the huge amount of offal derived from the salmon that are actually canned. Besides the salmon, great quantities of other fish, such as halibut, are caught in the nets and traps, and these are all wasted. During our stay at . . . [Stariski] a halibut got into the trap which was so large that before it could be taken out it had to be cut into four pieces. There are also great quantities of oulachan, or candle-fish, a small fish about the size of a smelt, and so full of oil that they are said to be capable of being lighted and used as a candle: hence their name. I have seen after a gale a strip several miles long and a couple of feet broad of these little fish lying one on top of the other along high water mark. All this fish surplus, however, goes to waste, but I should think before long, considering the value of fish manure in California, some enterprising company will start the manufacture of it on a large scale in Alaska. So far there seems to be no diminution in the number of salmon in Alaskan waters—they are still there in countless millions; but indiscriminate slaughter must tell its tale in the end, as it has done everywhere else.

The greater part of the actual work of canning is done by machinery, from the time the salmon makes his entrance into the building through a machine which deprives him of his head, tail, and fins, splits him open and eviscerates him, until he is converted into a row of shining 1 lb. tins labelled "Best Alaskan Red Salmon." All this part of the business is attended to by Chinamen. of whom about eighty are employed. . . . At times of great pressure, during the height of the run, they practically work all round the clock, as many as 1800 cases having been turned out in a single day. The cannery also employs about seventy white men, engineers, overseers, fishermen, &c., the great majority of the fishermen being Russian Finns. All this large colony goes south about the third week in August, when the place is left deserted, with the exception of a solitary caretaker, until the following April.

18

The Forgotten Shore in 1890

by Robert Porter

All through the winter the shores of the Kamishak are deserted and desolate, a wilderness of barren rock and drifting snow, the battlefield of furious gales, and trembling before the unceasing onslaught of a raging sea, kept in a state of turmoil by the joint action of wind and tide.

Below Tyonek, to Cape Douglas—excluding the shelter provided by Chisik Island where Snug Harbor is now located, and excluding the portage to Iliamna Lake—the western shore of Cook Inlet remained relatively untouched except by seasonal otter hunters and later, fishermen. Some of the reasons are mentioned in the Census of 1890. The Census bore Superintendent Robert Porter's byline but the reader may recognize the sharp pen of Ivan Petroff, who was never at a loss for words, even in the absence of evidence.

*P*roceeding in a southwesterly direction from the mouth of the Sushitna river, along the west coast of the inlet, we find the first settlement on the shores of a bight between North and West Foreland, named Traders bay. . . . The native inhabitants of this region, a branch of the Tnaina tribe, numbering between 150 and 200 people, subsist chiefly upon the proceeds of hunting and trapping, but since the establishment of salmon canneries they have been enabled to add considerably to their income by seining the magnificent king salmon that visit this part of the coast during the season. The cannery steam tenders call for the fish, and owing to competition the price paid the natives varies from 10 to 25 cents apiece. At Toyonok, near West Foreland, rival trading stores connected with the fisheries afford these Indians an opportunity to supply their wants at reasonable rates, while on the other hand the same competition secures them the highest prices for their furs. They are all members of the Russian orthodox church, and pay occasional visits to the mission church at Kenai.

In former times the Toyonok Tnainas acted as middlemen for the Sushitna branch of their tribe, but the latter now annually visit the station to trade, and to a limited extent share in the labor of fishing for the canneries. . . .

Kustatan, an isolated settlement of the same tribe, is located on the large bight south of West Foreland. It contains 45 people, who, besides hunting and trapping for land furs, engage in occasional expeditions in search of sea otters along the coast to the southward. The village stands upon a level tract of sandy soil, which, under Russian rule, was partially cultivated and furnished the best potatoes on Cook inlet. Left to themselves since the transfer of the country, the natives first neglected and finally abandoned this useful industry, and they now live by hunting and trapping, with dried fish as their staple winter's food. Both the hair seal and the grampus or white whale are hunted with canoes, but they are not captured in sufficient numbers to figure prominently in their domestic economy.

But one safe harbor exists on all this western coast of the inlet, in the deep indentation between Redoubt and Iliamna mountains. It is known as . . . [Chisik] harbor, and is protected from easterly winds by a small, high island. The cannery establishments of Kenai and Kassilof make use of this shelter to moor their large sailing vessels in safety during the season. Communication with the canneries is kept up by means of steam tenders. A salmon stream of limited capacity enters the head of this bay, and indications of the presence of mineral in the mountains are not wanting.

The low island of Kalgin, lying off this part of the coast, is not known to have been permanently inhabited within historic times, though traces of native dwellings exist. Up to comparatively recent times the natives from both sides of the inlet periodically visited the island to hunt hair seals and sea birds.

But a few miles to the southward of the . . . [Chisik] anchorage we find the bay of . . . [Chinitna], a deep indentation of the coast, but too shallow to serve as a harbor for any but the smallest sailing craft. This bay has been visited annually during the last decade by large sea-otter hunting parties of Kodiak Eskimo, numbering from 100 to 200 canoes, carried here by schooners or steamers of the Alaska Commercial Company, and taken home again with their spoils when supplies were exhausted. These hunters lived in temporary camps upon the low sandspits partially inclosing the bay, going to sea in search of otters whenever the weather was clear and the sea smooth enough for canoes. For many years this was the richest sea-otter hunting ground in the Kodiak district, but as from year to year the number of white men hunting with schooners of from 8 to 15 tons burden increased, until the surface of the inlet was dotted with their sails, the shy animals began to disappear, and the few which escaped from the incessant slaughter sought more retired feeding grounds.

No permanent settlement exists on the mainland from . . . [Chinitna] bay to and beyond Cape Douglas, the coast being bold and mountainous, and beset with outlying reefs dangerous to navigators. At Iliamna bay, which is shallow and affords but precarious shelter, we find a small depot of supplies for the trade with the Tnaina villages on Iliamna lake, to which the merchandise is carried on the backs of men over a steep mountain trail. On the island of St. Augustine, locally known as Chernobura, white men as well as natives can be found periodically hunting the sea otters which make the rocky reefs, extending seaward like the arms of a squid, a favorite resort.

More than 10 years ago a violent convulsion, accompanied by volcanic manifestations, caused quite a change in the outlines and topography of the island; a large crater appeared on its side, and the pyramidical summit fell in. At present only smoke and vapors issue from the crater and hundreds of lateral fissures. During the time of Russia's occupation the experiment was made of "planting" black foxes upon this island, but it met with failure. Subsequently a number of hogs were landed there to propagate, as it was thought that they would thrive upon the large quantities of mussels, clams, and seaweed, but the hogs perished during the first winter.

Along the shores of Kamishak bay, between St. Augustine island on the north and Cape Douglas on the south, numerous camps of sea-otter hunters can be found every season from early spring until late in autumn. These camps are occupied by . . . Eskimo, who, under instigation of traders, undertake long, tedious journeys, transporting their household goods and skin canoes on sledges over tundra, rivers, lakes, and mountain ranges, before the snow melts in the spring, to return only when the first storms of autumn make sleighing possible again. The Togiagmiut, whose villages are located far to the westward of Bristol bay, must cover between 200 and 300 miles in their journeys to this hunting ground. All through the winter the shores of the Kamishak are deserted and desolate, a wilderness of barren rock and drifting snow, the battlefield of furious gales, and trembling before the unceasing onslaught of a raging sea, kept in a state of turmoil by the joint action of wind and tide. But though the native hunter gladly turns his face homeward

115

on the approach of the dismal season, a few white men can be found to brave it. Small camps of otter hunters exist on the low, barren islands near the southern shore. Low structures of rocks, canvas, and drift logs are anchored with chains and cables to the rocky surface, to prevent them from being swept away before the constant gales; and here the hunter watches for weeks and months, bereft of all comforts, unable to stand erect within his lowly dwelling, while the force of the wind prevents him from doing so outside, waiting for a day's or even a few hours' lull between storms to visit his nets or to shoot sea otter from his boat.

19

The Coal Rush

by William Healey Dall

For the use of the small steam tug Kodat, *upon which we were traveling, our party broke out about 15 tons of this coal with crowbars, and we depended upon it entirely for steam purposes and galley fuel during the rest of the voyage to the Shumagins.*

The Russians had ignored Petr Doroshin's discovery of gold and decided instead to develop the coal resources of Cook Inlet. Their successors followed the same course. It was coal not gold that first attracted substantial American mining to the Inlet. The reader has already met Mr. W. T. Ballou and his correspondents, in the *Congressional Globe.* Many visitors to the north shore of Kachemak Bay, near Homer, reported the presence of coal, and passing ships occasionally used it as fuel. For example, according to William Healey Dall, "The coal was pronounced good by the engineers of Sir Thomas Hesketh's yacht *Lancashire Witch*, who used it for steaming purposes

117

in 1880, and also found it to burn well in an open grate in the cabin." Six years later, residents of the area organized the "Cleveland Mining District."

Here, Dall summarizes the coal mining activity, from the Russian effort to 1895. The mining continued after 1895, and at the turn of the century underground work was begun by the Cook Inlet Coal Fields Company, between Cooper and Coal creeks, at the present site of Homer. A narrow-gauge railroad connected the shafts to a dock at the end of Homer Spit. Coal mining in the region during all periods probably produced no more than a few thousand tons.

[P]ort Graham], also known as English Bay, was first described by Portlock in 1786, though it had previously been known to the Russians. Portlock says:

> We landed on the west side of the bay, and in walking around it discovered two veins of kennel coal situated near some hills just above the beach, about the middle of the bay, and with very little trouble several pieces were got out of the bank nearly as large as a man's head. . . . In the evening we returned on board and I tried some of the coal we had discovered and found it to burn clear and well.

Portlock made a chart of the bay, and named the cove under Dangerous Cape, where he saw the coal, "Coal Bay." He gives a view of the cove, in which, however, the height of the hills is much exaggerated. Later on the Russians established a trading post, which was called Alexandrovsk, on the opposite side of the bay. The presence of a large native village and the vicinity of the otter hunting grounds were probably the deciding reasons for this location. . . . About 1852 the Russian American Company began to make use of the steamers, and their attention was called to the coal described by Portlock and subsequently reported upon by Doroshin and Wossnessenski. Doroshin was a mining engineer detailed to examine the mineral resources of the colony, and under his supervision a shipload of the coal was obtained and taken to

119

San Francisco to be tested. The Russian American Company hesitated to undertake mining operations on its own account, and, having entered into relations with certain Californian capitalists, in 1852 an establishment at Kodiak was authorized by which the American Company was permitted to put up ice for the California market. After various tests had been made, the same company was empowered, on raising the necessary capital, to open the coal mines at Port Chatham.

In April, 1855, the bark *Cyane*, Captain Kinzie, left San Francisco for Port Chatham, where miners and mining machinery were landed. It is difficult at this date to obtain information in regard to these mining operations, which continued some ten years and supplied the Russians with a certain amount of coal which was used on their steamers. As better coal became available by the opening of mines in British Columbia, Oregon, and Puget Sound, the Port Chatham coal became less necessary, and with the transfer of the territory to the United States the mine was finally abandoned. The disturbed condition of the beds, already referred to, interrupted the mining operations by frequent faults, and it was complained that an excess of sulphur in the coal made it destructive to boiler tubes and grate bars. Nevertheless, like the Mount Diablo coal of California, which was even more objectionable, and for similar reasons, the Port Chatham coal for a time served a useful purpose. In 1880 I visited the site of the workings and found the tunnel inaccessible from the water which partially filled it and the caving in due to the rotting of the timbering. The works had evidently been of a primitive kind, as there were no permanent buildings and not even a pier for shipping the coal. Only a few pieces of worn-out, rusty machinery and the tunnel in the bluff at the top of the beach remained to show that any work had ever been attempted here. I have seen statements that an extensive stone pier and costly buildings had been erected here and large sums of money lost in the attempt to utilize the coal, but, apart from the intrinsic improbability of such foolish doings, no evidence of the truth of the statements was furnished by the locality itself at that time. . . . At present there is no coal visible at the surface, and in view of the better conditions prevalent to the northwest the existence of coal seams at Port Chatham has only an historical interest.

[On Kachemak Bay], immediately above the long [Homer] spit . . . are several seams close together, aggregating about 7 feet, separated by strata of leaf-bearing shale. The lowest of the coal seams is the best and thickest. This seam shows about 18 inches of clear coal, which is nearly the lowest of all seams exposed on this side of the bay, and runs from the bluff obliquely across the beach as far as it could be followed at low water. As nearly as could be determined, the average dip was about 15°N., but this changed and became less steep gradually along the seam. This seam is said to be the one explored in February, 1888, upon which the Alaska Coal Company's entry was founded, and on which a tunnel, now caved in, was run by Mr. J. A. Bradley, who has devoted much energy and some years of labor to the development of these mines. For convenience in discussing the different coal seams, I shall refer to this one as the Bradley seam. Its exact location is on the beach a short distance southwest of the mouth of a small river, the first which falls into the bay above the spit. . . .

The coal is more compact, more disposed to cubical fracture, and more glossy when broken than that of the geologically higher veins farther up the bay. For the use of the small steam tug *Kodat,* upon which we were traveling, our party broke out about 15 tons of this coal with crowbars, and we depended upon it entirely for steam purposes and galley fuel during the rest of the voyage to the Shumagins. The shore in front of the mine, as is the case the whole length of the bay, runs off shoal for a mile or more, which is dry at low water, the range of tide in the bay sometimes exceeding 30 feet. Under present conditions coal can be lightered off only at favorable stages of the tide. Near the eastern end of the spit, however, deep water comes close to the beach with a perfectly protected anchorage, and the plans for utilizing the coal of this bay which I have heard discussed have almost uniformly included a railway out upon the spit to the deep water referred to. This is obviously the most convenient plan, and would greatly reduce the amount of wharf which otherwise would have to be constructed. Of course any corporation which owned the spit would possess great advantages over any other shippers of coal. Mr. Bradley states that the teredo, so destructive at Sitka and other points in Alaska, is not found in the bay, and I observed no traces of its work on driftwood, etc. If this exemption is a permanent one, it will be of a good deal of importance from a pecuniary standpoint.

Proceeding northeastward, the bluffs which form the northern shore are from time to time interrupted by the canyons of small streams which enter the bay obliquely to the shore line, almost all of them trending inland to the north or eastward of north. At their mouths narrow strips of beach land are found; almost everywhere else the sea at high water comes up to the foot of the bluffs. The steep sides of these canyons give good sections of the strata to the prospector, and of these advantage has been taken. Three of them are the site of prospective coal mines on which some exploration has been done. There are in all some half dozen principal canyons, besides some smaller ones. the southernmost locality where mining has been done is called McNeil Canyon. . . .

Beginning to the westward and working up the bay, at a point a few hundred yards southwest of McNeil Canyon, Mr. Curtis has run two short tunnels into the bluff about 45 feet above the beach. The clear coal is here 4 feet 7 inches thick, with about 6 inches of iron-stained sandstone above it and a thick, adhesive, gray clay below. This seam would require timbering, to avoid caving in, if worked to any extent. Above this are three other seams, separated by thick beds of clay or soft sandstone. One of these, the lower seam, is nearly 4 feet thick; the others are somewhat thinner. The strata are here nearly horizontal. . . .

From McNeil Canyon, next above, in 1891, Lieut. R. P. Schwerin, U.S.N., on behalf of New York parties, prospected for coal, and took out 200 tons of it, which was taken to San Francisco and in September, 1891, was submitted to a series of tests. . . . This expedition left no permanent works or buildings.

The next locality is the Cottonwood Canyon, where some prospecting has been done and a log house built at the delta as a shelter for the prospectors and to hold the location. The exploration here has not proceeded far.

Next above is Eastland Canyon, where more work has been done than at any other single locality on the bay. The engineer in charge, Mr. M. B. Curtis, offered us every hospitality in his power, and showed us everything which was to be seen.

A small tramway leads back several hundred yards into the canyon, and at a height of 270 feet above the tide we found a vein 2 feet 4 inches thick of clear coal, and associated with it alternate smaller seams of coal and clay, or "bone," the total thickness of the series being 6 feet. The rocks here are nearly horizontal, and comprise sandstone, whitish clay containing large waterworn bowlders, shales, and lignite, the upper part covered with from 5 to 10 feet of reddish gravel. The bluffs attain a height of from 600 to 800 feet, the land behind them reaching 1,800 feet. These explorations were begun in December, 1894, by the North Pacific Mining and Transportation Company, under the supervision of Mr. Curtis. About 300 tons had been taken out and sent to San Francisco for trial, and another cargo was to be shipped shortly after our visit. Mr. Curtis had only a few men employed, and the work he was doing was of the nature of exploration. The development of the property, he stated, would depend upon the results of experiments with the coal.

The parties actively interested at present in these coal deposits are two corporations. The older is the Alaska Coal Company, incorporated December 26, 1889, under the laws of California, with a capital stock of $2,000,000, distributed among 89 stockholders in shares of a par value of $10 each. . . . They have expended about $50,000 in exploration. The other corporation is the North Pacific Mining and Transportation Company, organized under the laws of California in October, 1894. . . . The expenditure of this company to October, 1895, aggregated $42,000, and I was verbally informed that 650 tons of coal in all had been taken out from the works at Eastland Canyon.

I received the impression that these two corporations, if not composed of the same members throughout, were at least not competitors, and were sustained chiefly by capital from a common source.

A test made by the Southern Pacific Company was of the nature of an investigation into the utility of the coal for railway purposes. It was, I am informed, determined that the liability of the coal, while burning under a forced draft, to throw off large ignited cinders, made it, if used for railway purposes, dangerous to crops and buildings in so dry a country as California in summer, and this disqualification was decisive.

The two coal companies above described claim at present the long spit and the whole northern shore of Kachemak Bay inside the spit, under various laws or usages. If the bay should become the site of mining operations, a light-house would be needed on the extremity of the spit, and it would therefore be advisable to reserve from entry a certain portion, at least, for Government uses. So far as buildings are concerned, those at present standing are: (1) A house, store, and several outbuildings at the end of the spit, which I was informed were the property of Mr. Bradley, or the Alaska Coal Company, of which he is a member, and which were unoccupied at the time of our visit; (2) a number of buildings at the foot of the bluff near the other end of the spit . . . where it joins the mainland. These are unoccupied and out of repair; they are nominally in charge of Mr. Cooper, of Ninilchik, who visits them occasionally, and are the property of the Alaska Coal Company.

The North Pacific Mining and Transportation Company has two or three buildings, a tramway, and a short pier at the mouth of Eastland Canyon, and houses at the mouth of Cottonwood and McNeil canyons. They also have one or more lighters at the cove named Bear Cove, on the opposite side of the bay, which is better protected than the north shore. These buildings were occupied by Mr. Curtis and his force of employees at the time of our visit. All these houses are log or frame structures, sufficiently substantial for their purposes.

20

The Other Rush in 1896-1898

by Walter C. Mendenhall

. . . here, as in other parts of Alaska, the operator must work in very much richer ground than would be necessary in the States in order to make mining pay.

Among white traders the members of this small [Matanuska] band are regarded with more or less suspicion. A few years since one of their number murdered the storekeeper at Knik and was promptly hanged for it by the latter's associates.

Coal mining at the end of the nineteenth century was further stimulated by the sudden appearance of a local market for fuel. In 1896, the year of George Carmack's strike on the Klondike, Cook Inlet was already the scene of a small gold rush to the northeastern Kenai Peninsula and to the north beach of Turnagain Arm. Walter C. Mendenhall (later Director of the U.S. Geological Survey) was assigned in 1898 to an Army expedition sent to explore travel routes northward from the Inlet. He described the economic geology of the gold district, and some of the effects of white immigration on the native inhabitants.

Since 1896, when the first considerable influx of miners reached the Cook Inlet region in response to the strike made on Sixmile Creek during the previous year, [the Sunrise District] has been fairly well known as a mining center, and has attracted a modest share of the Alaskan immigration each season.

Previous to 1896 gold had been mined for two or three years on Bear Creek, a tributary of Resurrection Creek, and colors were found in all the streams thereabout, but the district was not well known and had been prospected but little.

Since 1896 more systematic work has been done by the few among the usual throng of prospectors who have any idea of such work, and most of the streams which enter Turnagain Arm have been examined more or less thoroughly to their sources. As a result the productive parts of the district have been extended from Bear Creek to include other tributaries of Resurrection Creek, most of Sixmile and its branches, and, on the north side of the arm, Bird Creek and Glacier Creek.

Work has as yet not been generally carried across the divide north of Turnagain Arm, although one or two claims were staked on Knik drainage in 1898, because the region in this direction is difficult of access and prospectors are usually without pack animals.

Within the peninsula, south of Turnagain Arm, some prospecting has been done along Kenai lake and river, and during

1898 one or two expensive attempts were made to develop hydraulic properties here.

Hope City, at the mouth of Resurrection Creek, was at first the leading camp of the district, but with the more rapid development of the Sixmile diggings Sunrise City, at the mouth of this stream, became the larger town and is now the center of distribution for the region.

So far only placer work has been done, and this has been confined to the short summer season of about three months, when the year's wages must be made, so that here, as in other parts of Alaska, the operator must work in very much richer ground than would be necessary in the States in order to make mining pay.

Mills Creek, Canyon Creek, and probably the other branches of Sixmile Creek have their sources in the gravel sheet which buries the broad divides in this part of the peninsula. These gravels are coarse or fine, rudely stratified, and are here always of local derivation; that is, practically the only rocks in them are fragments of the slates, arkoses, and associated quartz veins and acid dikes which constitute the Sunrise series. They were probably distributed as aprons along the front of the valley glaciers as they retreated after the last advance, and appear to have been deposited near sea level. But the ice streams at that time occupied about the same basins as are now drained by the creeks and their tributaries, so that, except for their great extent, these fluvioglacial gravels do not differ from those of exclusively fluvial origin. It is not likely that the gold was well concentrated in the gravels when they were first deposited, because of the rapidity of their deposition and the probability that ice was the chief carrier. This inference is borne out by the fact that fairly heavy colors can be panned from the gravels in the undisturbed terraces at almost any point. But with the birth of the present streams and the elevation of the land to or nearly to its present position concentration began. The creeks cutting down through the gold-bearing gravels acted exactly like sluices on a large scale, and where the cutting has reached bed rock the gold content of all the removed gravels is found. This makes the rich ground which has yielded the best returns in the district—as, for instance, on the property of the Polly Mining Company along the lower course of Mills Creek. . . .

Although at present the best-paying properties within the district are in streams which derive their gravels from the general gravel sheet, others are supplied in the usual way—directly from the rocks forming the stream bed and valley walls. Among the streams in this latter class may be mentioned Bear Creek and Glacier Creek. The chief difference between the two types of streams is to be found in the fact that those which are cutting through the old gravels generally derive their gold from a somewhat greater area than those which act directly upon bed rock. In both cases the gravels are of local origin.

During the summers of 1897 and 1898 some work was done on the tributaries of Kenai River and the streams which flow into the lower end of Lake Kenai. Cooper Creek and its western branch, Stetson Creek, were reported to contain the richest diggings in this part of the peninsula, and contain perhaps the only ground there carrying gold enough to pay for sluicing. Fairly good indications are reported, also, from some of the eastern tributaries of Lake Kenai. . . .

Bird Creek, which enters Turnagain Arm opposite the mouth of Sixmile Creek, has attracted considerable attention for a year or two past, and is believed by those familiar with the district to hold some paying claims, although upon development many have proved disappointing to their owners.

Crow Creek, a tributary of Glacier, promises well and is now being developed by the claim owners. Preliminary work has shown rather coarse gold, a $50 nugget from this stream having been brought into Sunrise during July.

In the spring of 1898 the Alaskan Hydraulic Syndicate brought a hydraulic outfit to the gravel banks about the lower end of Kenai Lake, where prospects appeared favorable. By autumn the managers had satisfied themselves that the gravel, of which there was an unlimited amount in sight, was not rich enough for profitable manipulation, and withdrew. Their property occupied the north bank of Kenai River about the mouth of Juneau Creek, which enters the river but a short distance below the lake. Some gravel banks along Sixmile and Canyon creeks show good indications, and it is to be hoped that they will be developed in the near future. They belong to the older, the fluvioglacial series of gravels, which have been sluiced by Mills Creek and Canyon Creek.

An attempt was made during the past summer to develop the gravels along the beach on the west shore of Cook Inlet between

Tyonek and Ladds Station, but the experiment ended in commercial disaster.

Some quartz properties have been staked in the district, but have not been developed. Near the mouth of Sawmill Creek, which flows into the south side of the Arm, a few miles above Sunrise, a ledge of doubtful extent is reported. On Bird Creek, a property for whose richness most extravagant claims were made, was located by one of the local prospectors. A sample, given to the writer, proved to be a fragment of one of the aplite dikes so numerous in the Sunrise series. It assayed about $7.50 per ton, mostly in gold.

On the whole, it may be said that few of the claims about Turnagain Arm are profitable. The shortness of the season for work here, as in other parts of Alaska, is an element in bringing about this result. Less than $5 per day to the man during the working season of about three months will scarcely pay the prospectors' expenses during the long idle period. The Mills Creek property has paid in its richest parts as high as $120 per day to the man for short periods, but this is a maximum very rarely reached. The series of 5 claims included in this property yield a revenue of about $25,000 a year and are regarded as the best properties within the district. Many placers which are worked pay less than $3 per day and are disposed of by the owners as quickly as possible. The only mining so far done is placer work. The outlook for paying quartz is not good, but conditions seem favorable for profitable hydraulic work in a few localities.

* * *

The native inhabitants of the region about the head of Cook Inlet belong to the true Indian stock, as distinguished from the Eskimo tribes of the coast. They are now collected into a few small villages, as at Tyonek, Ladds Station, and Knik, where their original customs have been much modified by white traders, upon whom they are becoming more and more dependent. Physically they are slight and will average less in stature than the whites. They are good-natured, timid, disinclined to quarrel, and are generally honest, although idlers. They still depend in a measure upon the summer's catch of salmon to keep them from starvation during the winter season, but secure clothing of white manufacture and many articles of food from the stores of the various trading companies in exchange for furs. Their winter habitations are rude cabins, which are sometimes occupied throughout the summer months also, but are quite as often discarded for tents until severe weather begins again.

Pulmonary and inherited diseases are making constant inroads on their numbers, particularly at the stations, where their native customs have been most modified by white influence. The Indians of Knik, for instance, are much more robust than those at Ladds Station.

The Matanuskas dwell about the southern edge of the Copper River Plateau, generally on Copper River drainage. They are more active than the coast tribes and are held in much awe by them. Once or twice during each winter season they come down the Matanuska River on the ice to exchange their furs with the traders at the head of Knik Arm for firearms, ammunition, clothing, or food. The journey of more than 100 miles is usually very leisurely performed and occupies several weeks. At such times the women and children are often left behind, very scantily provided for, and the supplies purchased from the traders are usually consumed before the braves reach their homes again. Among white traders the members of this small band are regarded with more or less suspicion. A few years since one of their number murdered the storekeeper at Knik and was promptly hanged for it by the latter's associates. The lesson seems to have been effective and no further trouble has occurred.

The Matanuskas penetrate the Sushitna Basin, at least to the upper waters of the Talkeetna, one of their caribou hunting grounds, and also meet the Lower Copper Indians to the east. There are probably not 100 of them all told. ▓

21

Petroleum on the West Shore, 1882-1906

by Fred H. Moffitt

. . . this well . . . was said to be more than 1,000 feet deep, that gas was encountered all the way below 190 feet, and that considerable oil was found at a depth of either 500 or 700 feet.

The presence of petroleum near Cook Inlet was detected long before the modern Kenai wells were brought into production. One petroleum claim was staked as early as 1892, and drilling was underway around the turn of the century, during the coal and gold rushes. A geologist describes the first Alaskan oil fever.

133

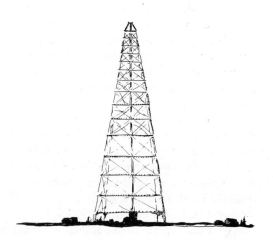

*T*he area described in this paper is on the west side of Cook Inlet between Iniskin and Chinitna Bays. It is a peninsula that has an area of about 130 square miles and is separated from the mainland mountains on the west by a narrow valley which extends from the Right Arm of Iniskin Bay northeastward to the head of Chinitna Bay. . . . Oil Bay [is] on the south side of the peninsula. . . . Seldovia, on the southwest end of Kenai Peninsula, is directly across Cook Inlet from Chinitna Bay and is the nearest white settlement and the nearest post office except that at Iliamna, a native village on Iliamna Lake.

The west coast of Cook Inlet has never had more than a scanty white population. It does not abound in fur-bearing animals, has not attracted many prospectors for the metals, and, until recently has had no canneries. The vicinity of Oil Bay, however, at one time received considerable attention because of the petroleum seepages found there and was the scene of drilling for a number of years. Shortly before the Alaskan oil lands were withdrawn from entry in 1910, the oil properties were abandoned, and no further attention was paid to them until the new leasing law was passed in 1920. This law renewed interest in the district, so that much of the ground was restaked, and it accordingly became necessary, in order to carry out the provisions of the law, to collect information regarding the areal geology and structure of the area likely to be prospected for oil.

* * *

[G. C.] Martin states that indications of petroleum were discovered in the Iniskin Bay region in 1853 and that the first samples of petroleum were taken by a Russian named Paveloff in 1882. A man named Edelman staked claims near the heads of Bowser and Brown Creeks in 1892, but these claims were not drilled and apparently no work of any kind was done on them. Pomeroy & Griffen staked claims near the head of Oil Bay in 1896, organized the Alaska Petroleum Co. in 1897, and began preliminary work on the ground in 1898. Drilling is reported to have been in progress in 1900, although [F. H.] Oliphant says that the well at Oil Bay was started in 1902, after unsuccessful attempts had been made in 1899 to land machinery and in 1901 to begin drilling. Work on the first well, half a mile from the bay, near Bowser Creek was ended in 1903.

Martin was unable to get authentic information about this well but states that it was said to be more than 1,000 feet deep, that gas was encountered all the way below 190 feet, and that considerable oil was found at a depth of either 500 or 700 feet. It seems improbable that the reported flow of 50 barrels a day was actually obtained, although oil was undoubtedly present. When the well was drilled deeper a strong flow of salt water shut off the flow of oil. Efforts to recover the oil or to drill deeper were not successful. At present water flows from the pipe and through it gas bubbles continually, but practically no oil accompanies it.

A second hole was drilled in 1904 near the base of a hill three-tenths of a mile northwest of the first well and nearly 400 feet north of the road to Iniskin Bay. When this well had reached a depth of 450 feet it was abandoned because of caving shale. The log of the well [was] furnished by Mr. August Bowser, who had charge of the drilling. . . .

A third well was started in the same year almost directly south of the second well and about 150 feet from the road. It was sunk to a depth of 900 feet but was cased for only 630 feet. Caving ground was encountered at 830 feet. At 770 feet three oil sands 6 to 8 inches thick and 4 or 5 feet apart were passed through. According to Mr. Bowser the well produced about 10 barrels of oil a day and had a gas pressure sufficient to blow water into the derrick to a height of 20 feet.

Water now flows from the pipe in this well but in less amount than from the first well. A little gas and oil also came up the pipe with the water, but the quantity is less than that in the natural seepage at the foot of the hill a short distance to the east.

A fourth hole was started on the low hill half a mile north of the cabin at the first hole. The derrick is still standing. No information concerning this hole is at hand. The pipe was plugged, and no evidence of oil, gas, or water was seen when the place was visited in 1921. No drilling was done at Oil Bay after 1906, and in 1909 the claims were abandoned.

Drilling operations at Dry Bay were undertaken by the Alaska Oil Co. at about the same time as at Oil Bay. This company was organized in 1901 and began drilling in 1902. The first well was put down that year, but the tools were lost at a depth of 320 feet without obtaining oil, and the hole was abandoned. The well had a diameter of 8 inches to a depth of 212 feet and of 6 inches below that depth. A second well was started in 1903 near the first but was soon abandoned because of an accident to the machinery. ▓

22

Farming the Subarctic Frontier in 1898

by C. C. Georgeson

We have made hay from the same land year after year for twelve years, and never planted any grain, as the native grass has grown on the ground from which we make the hay without our aid.

The gold rushes revived national interest in Alaska. In addition to federal explorers and geologists, the government sent agricultural scientists to the north country. One, C. C. Georgeson, investigated the agricultural possibilities at several locations in the Territory. His reports revealed that agriculture in Alaska was not as hopeless as congressional critics of the purchase had argued in 1868.

*G*rain and forage plants have not been tested with sufficient care elsewhere in the Territory to warrant a positive statement that they will grow there, but vegetables and in some places berry plants have been tested more or less carefully at nearly every settlement in Alaska, and, to indicate what success growers have achieved, brief quotations from a few of the reports received on this subject are made.

* * *

Eugene R. Bogart, of Kenai, writes as follows: "At Kenai, 10 miles north of [Kasilof], gardens can be seen, with peas, cabbage, tomatoes, turnips, ruta-bagas, radishes, lettuce, celery, beets, onions, and hills of potatoes, covering in all several acres. There never has been any trouble in raising garden truck at this place, the main difficulty being the poverty of the people and also the getting of seed to plant. . . . At Ninilchik, a village midway between [Kasilof] and Anchor Point, are at least 20 acres under cultivation. The principal products are potatoes, turnips, cabbage, and lettuce, but all kinds of vegetables have been raised there."

Anderson Brothers write from Pearl [Perl] Island, at the entrance to Cook Inlet, and incidentally mention the efforts at gardening by the natives: "The natives, seeing us raising potatoes and other vegetables, started in to raise some themselves, with surprising results. The implement they use in working the ground is generally a barrel stave or other stick of wood. This year most of them have a little garden, but our garden seed did not reach to all. The turnip is held the most easily raised of all garden products. They often grow to the size of a dinner plate in circumference. The native is a willing gardener. They have found that vegetables, along with salmon, save the flour sack a great deal. The commercial seeds found in this country are very unreliable, and if the Department would distribute some seed among the natives, I do not doubt that they would be thoroughly tested. We plant potatoes in May and harvest them the latter part of September or the beginning of October, according to the season. One box of seed potatoes will produce four boxes of as large potatoes as any raised in California and one box of small, immature potatoes."

* * *

Cattle were introduced by the Russians in their various settlements, and according to reports they always did well. It is certainly a fact that the cattle which are now found at the little towns along the coast look well during the summer while on pasture, and they appear to have become adapted to the climate. Family cows are kept by many of the white settlers, and one or more dairymen may also be found at nearly every town. The writer took occasion to examine these cattle whenever it was possible, and to look into the methods and cost of feeding. Grades of various breeds were represented. At Juneau the shorthorn type predominated; at Sitka, high-grade Jerseys; while at Kodiak and in the Cook Inlet region Holstein-Friesian grades were most common, with a sprinkling of some small dun-colored cattle with upright horns, said to be of Siberian origin and to be a remnant of the cattle kept by the Russians during their occupancy. . . .

The excellent condition of the cattle bore evidence to the nutritious quality of the indigenous grasses. On this point it is of interest to quote from reports made to the writer by men from various parts of the Territory who have had experience in cattle raising.

* * *

Rev. Ivan Bortnovsky, from Kenai, says: "In regard to stock raising, I can say from experience that my cattle are in a splendid condition, healthy, and, from feed which is obtained in this neighborhood, as plump as cattle which are stall fed in other localities. Alfalfa, timothy, and oat hay can be grown here with great success. Barley, wheat, and other grain hay, from the shortness of the season and the abundant rainfall, become coarse, so cattle will not eat it."

Mr. A. S. Tibbey, of Coal Harbor, makes the following statement: "We have made hay from the same land year after year for twelve years, and never planted any grain, as the native grass has grown on the ground from which we make the hay without our aid. In making hay we cut it, then spread it out to dry, and the next day take it into the barn perfectly cured, and it keeps all winter. . . . From an experience of twelve years I think the country adapted for stock raising. Grass and water is abundant, and in winter the dry grass seems to retain its nutriment, as all the stock we have had seem to enjoy it. The snow does not lie on the ground for any length of time, and cattle can pick up most of their feed all winter."

23

Flora (1900)

by *Wilfred H. Osgood*

*The foliage of many of the smaller plants . . ., is bright
red, and adds greatly to the general effect. On the whole,
it reminds one very much of the autumn woods of New
England, and is quite unlike anything I have seen
elsewhere in Alaska.*

During the summer of 1900, Wilfred Osgood and Edmund
Heller of the U.S. Biological Survey stopped briefly at
Seldovia, Homer, Kenai and Sunrise, then spent two weeks near Hope
and two weeks near Tyonek studying the flora and fauna. Said Osgood:
"The region about Cook Inlet was, at the beginning of the field season
of 1900, the only general district of consequence on the Pacific coast of
Alaska that had not been recently visited by naturalists."

*V*ery little natural history work has been done in the Cook Inlet region. In 1869, Ferdinand Bischoff made a small collection of birds and mammals at Fort Kenai which was sent to the U.S. National Museum; but though casual references to individual specimens have occasionally appeared, no account of the collection, as a whole, has been published. The entire collection is recorded in the catalogues of the Museum, but many of the specimens have been exchanged or distributed to educational institutions; enough still remain, however, to be of considerable value in making a faunal list. A few species of birds from Cook Inlet have been recorded by Dr. Tarleton H. Bean, who made brief stops about the mouth of the inlet while connected with an expedition of the U.S. Coast and Geodetic Survey, and the specimens collected are deposited in the U.S. National Museum. A few specimens were also taken near the mouth of the inlet by Messrs. C. H. Townsend and B. W. Evermann during a brief stop of the U.S. Fish Commission steamer *Albatross*. Numerous sportsmen have, in recent years, been attracted by the large game in the vicinity of the inlet and in some cases have published accounts of their trips containing many valuable notes on the natural history and general features of the region. The most prominent of these are Messrs. Dall De Weese and Andrew J. Stone. Mr. De Weese collected and preserved an excellent series of moose and Dall sheep for the U.S. National Museum, and Mr.

147

Stone secured many fine specimens, including the type of *Rangifer stonei* [caribou], for the American Museum of Natural History, New York.

* * *

The flora of the Cook Inlet region is quite different in its general character from that of the coast farther south, although many species are common to both regions. The difference is largely in the reduction of the number of coniferous trees in the Cook Inlet region and the corresponding increase in deciduous trees; but other features somewhat transitional between the heavy saturated forest of the southern coast and the treeless tundra of the north are numerous. The flora of the mountainous district about Turnagain Arm is, of course, different from that of the coastal plains of other parts of the inlet. The low country near Hope consists of a grassy tide flat, about 50 acres in extent, and a few miles of forest and occasional small swamps along the lower part of Resurrection Creek. Balsam poplars, paper birches, alders, and willows abound near the streams, and spruces and hemlocks are common on the slopes and slightly elevated flats. A third species of spruce is found in the small peat bogs, where smaller Hudsonian plants, such as Labrador tea, crowberry, and dwarf birch are in profusion. The hemlock is much the most abundant of the large trees, but it is exceeded in individual size by the spruces. The conifers ascend the mountain slopes to about 2,000 feet but above that point rapidly disappear. Beyond this elevation are alder thickets, small patches of dwarf willows and birches, and vast stretches of waving grass from 1 to 3 feet high. Still higher, the slopes and rounded backs of the ridges are cushioned with a mass of heather and heather-like shrubs. . . . This extends up to an approximate altitude of 5,000 feet, above which there is very little or no plant growth. The whole country is characterized by the abundance of high grass; otherwise it is a typical Hudsonian-Alpine region.

The flora on the northwest side of the inlet in the vicinity of Tyonek is somewhat different in character. With the exception of considerable areas occupied by lakes and peat bogs, the whole country is covered with comparatively open forest. Deciduous trees greatly outnumber conifers, of which but two species occur, and one of these is quite rare and local. The paper birch is by far the most abundant tree, and next in rank are the poplars, of which there are two species. Alders and willows are found along the streams and sparingly through the forest. The underbrush is not heavy; it consists mainly of *Menziesia* and . . . [high bush cranberry], with an occasional clump of devil's club in wet places. Long grass grows luxuriantly in numerous pretty open glades in the birch woods.

The September aspect of the forest is very attractive. From a little distance the birches on the low, rolling slopes appear as a mass of golden and rusty yellow, punctured here and there by the dark-green spruce tops. The foliage of many of the smaller plants, such as . . . [cranberry, bunchberry, currant and fireweed], is bright red, and adds greatly to the general effect. On the whole, it reminds one very much of the autumn woods of New England, and is quite unlike anything I have seen elsewhere in Alaska.

24

Headhunting Among the Forget-me-nots in 1902

by Colonel Claude Cane

Never have I seen anywhere such a wealth of wild flowers as I saw in this land, which I had always imagined to be one of the roughest and most inhospitable on the surface of the globe.

. . . the Government were well advised to impose restrictions on . . . indiscriminate slaughter [of moose], as it would be an enormous pity if these magnificent animals were to share the fate of the buffalo; and the case of these latter animals has shown how hard it is to get up a decent head of any species of wild animal again once it has been practically exterminated.

In the early twentieth century, among the unofficial visitors who were lured northward by gold rush stories and reports of Alaska's wilderness beauty, were a number of big game hunters. A few posed as amateur scientists and (as Wilfred Osgood contended), they occasionally contributed to our knowledge of natural history. Others came only to obtain animal trophies. It was the time when Theodore Roosevelt advocated federal policies to conserve American natural resources, while he himself shot up a volley whenever he was near the wild creatures of the world.

Another Colonel, an Englishman named Claude Cane, arrived in the Inlet during the summer of 1902, in pursuit of sporting adventure. He was a careful observer and a fine writer who exhibited the same Rooseveltian ambivalence toward nature. The Colonel also welcomed big game management. He returned to Britain with eight Dall sheep heads; the sheep was, he said, "one of the handsomest . . . game animals I have ever seen."

$\mathcal{N}$ature in these latitudes tries to make up for the short summer by being very bountiful with the floral treasures she heaps with lavish hand on the smiling country which it is difficult to believe was only a few weeks ago buried under a shroud of snow and ice four feet thick, beneath which the fertile earth had slept for eight long months. Here along the sandy shore were acres and acres of tall wild rye, mixed with wild peas whose dark blue flowers supplied a vivid note of colour, while the meadows were starred with countless white and purple daisies, bluebells, buttercups, larkspur, purple lupines, and yellow sunflowers, and the banks of every piece of water fringed by purple iris and forget-me-nots, with yellow water-lilies floating placidly on the surface of the pools. Never have I seen anywhere such a wealth of wild flowers as I saw in this land, which I had always imagined to be one of the roughest and most inhospitable on the surface of the globe. Truly, if it were not for the thrice-accursed mosquitos and sandflies, the shores of Cook's Inlet during the summer months would be a veritable Garden of Eden, and without the serpent too, as there is not such a thing in the whole length and breadth of the land.

But every rose has its thorn, and the Alaskan mosquitos, despite the beauty of the climate and country, go far towards making life positively unendurable. I cannot say, like some travellers, that I have seen them as big as snipe, nor have I amused myself by shooting them with a six-shooter, but I will say that they are the largest, most bloodthirsty, and most pertinacious of their species I have ever had the misfortune to encounter. It is not so much the bites—one gets acclimatised to them—but the incessant annoyance and irritation day and night. A veil worn loosely, so that it does not touch one's face, defeats them; but I have often had to take my veil off and brush or shake it, so thickly had they settled upon it, that it was impossible to see.

* * *

The Alaskan moose is several sizes bigger than his brother of Eastern and Middle Canada, and carries proportionately bigger antlers, as regards weight, span, and breadth of palmation. Indeed, he is to the Eastern moose much as the latter is to the Scandinavian elk. On the Kenai peninsula, at least, he is said never to "yard up" in the winter. Twenty years ago there was not, so the natives say, a single moose on the peninsula; but at about that date they began to cross the narrow isthmus at the head of Turnagain Arm, and the place has evidently been so much to their liking that, despite the numbers that are annually killed for meat by the natives, and by the miners at Sunrise and Hope City, they are increasing in numbers every year and seem to be in no immediate danger of extinction, or, indeed, of any serious diminution of numbers.

At the same time I think the Government were well advised to impose restrictions on their indiscriminate slaughter, as it would be an enormous pity if these magnificent animals were to share the fate of the buffalo; and the case of these latter animals has shown how hard it is to get up a decent head of any species of wild animals again once it has been practically exterminated. The two great sources of danger are meat-hunting and killing for the sake of procuring heads for the taxidermists and dealers in the States. The former cannot be controlled, but traffic in heads should be vigorously suppressed. The sportsman shooting for museums or his own private collection will do little or no harm, but all the same he ought not to be allowed to shoot without a licence, and the number of licenses should be limited. The size that the antlers of these mooose sometimes attain may be imagined when I say that I have seen many specimens spanning between 70 in. and 75 in., and that there is a well-known specimen, which was at any rate until a short time ago in the possession of a Chicago dealer, which spanned before it left Kenai no less than 81 in. . . .

The Alaskan white sheep (*Ovis Dalli*) was first . . . [reported] by Mr. E. W. Nelson in 1884, and named by him after Professor Dall, one of the first scientific explorers of Alaska. It occupies the most northerly range of any wild sheep in the world, extending from the Liard River on the south up to some distance inside the Arctic Circle, being very numerous in Cook's Inlet, especially on the Kenai peninsula. It is smaller than the brown sheep of the Rockies (*Ovis Canadensis*), generally known as the bighorn, and its horns are not so massive, but what it lacks in size it makes up for in grace, and is one of the handsomest and most sporting game animals I have ever seen. Their horns rarely exceed 15 in. in circumference at the base, though I have heard of 16 in. heads from the neighbourhood of Mount McKinley. My eight measured respectively, 14½ in., 14 in. (3), 13¾ (2), 13½ (2), and were a good average lot. They live altogether above timber line, amid the wildest surroundings, and their successful stalking and shooting entails a certain amount of hard work, for which the shooter is amply repaid by the glorious sport and the beauty of the surroundings.

* * *

Both natives and white explorers have all sorts of tales of white and other curiously coloured bears of huge size which they have met with in inaccessible places in the interior, but most of these accounts must be taken *cum grano*. All the varieties of brown bears have an evil reputation for savageness and ferocity, and are said to be worse in this respect than the grizzlies; but I expect that it is a case of six of one and half a dozen of the other, and that a wounded member of either family can be ugly enough if treated without the respect to which he is entitled.

I have met several men who have been more or less mauled, including Edelmann, the skipper of our sloop, who was laid out by a bear he followed into thick brush, and I have heard of many more cases, both of mutilation and death; but I suspect that in every one the catastrophe was due to the carelessness or foolhardiness of the sufferer. A man armed with a good repeating rifle has nothing to fear from a bear in the open, as long as he keeps his head and doesn't get "rattled"; but, of course, if he does, or if he is foolish enough to get tangled up with one in thick covert, he pays the penalty. . . .

On . . . [one] occasion I was coming home alone, having left . . . [my companions] on the high ground looking for caribou tracks, when I came on some tracks which led down to a bear trail through the alders. . . . I was using . . . [the trail] for convenience in getting through the bush, when, at the entrance of a clump of alders, I suddenly almost stepped on a brown she-bear and two cubs. The lady immediately showed fight, and I as immediately bolted into the open, where I sat down some twenty yards away, with both barrels of my Paradox cocked, awaiting a charge which never came off, as she preferred retreating, though growling in the most blood-curdling manner. If I had fired at her in the thick stuff I might have got her; but, on the other hand, she might have got me, and, as I was seven or eight miles from camp and all alone, if I had been only wounded I might have never been found, and might have, after days of pain, left my bones to whiten on the hillside.

If she had come after me into the open, I should have got two heavy bullets into her before she could get at me, and the chances would have been all in my favour. As it was, perhaps I was a coward, and perhaps I lost a bear I might have got; but I think I exercised a wise discretion.

25

To the
Oregon Robin
in Alaska (1899)

by John Burroughs

One headhunter came to Alaska three years earlier, in 1899, traveling in a grand style that has never been duplicated in the Alaskan tourist industry. Edward H. Harriman, the railroad potentate, chartered the steamer *George W. Elder* and bundled aboard the ship his family, a personal staff, several hunters, tons of supplies (including a library), and a platoon of distinguished naturalists, including: John Muir, William Dall, Henry Gannett, C. Hart Merriam, Bernard Fernow and George Bird Grinnell. The expedition was in Cook Inlet one day only, dropping anchor behind the hamlet of Homer at the end of Homer Spit. Said John Burroughs, the nature writer: "There was nothing

Homeric in the look of the place. . . ." Burroughs did rave about the town's natural setting, noting the grandeur of the mountains, especially Iliamna which "was wrapped in a mantle of snow, but . . . was evidently warm at heart, for we could see steam issuing from two points near its summit." His poem to the Oregon robin was written shortly thereafter at Kodiak, and fits here, for varied thrushes are plentiful along the Inlet. Burroughs did not see a "purple grosbeak" or a cedar tree, but of "loquacious ravens clacking and croaking" there is no shortage at Kodiak or on Cook Inlet.

O Varied thrush! O Robin strange!
  Behold my mute surprise.
Thy form and flight I long have known,
  But not this new disguise.

I do not know thy slaty coat,
  Nor vest with darker zone;
I'm puzzled by thy recluse ways
  And song in monotone.

I left thee 'mid my orchard's bloom,
  When May had crowned the year;
Thy nest was on the apple bough,
  Where rose thy carol clear.

Thou lurest now through fragrant shades,
  Where hoary spruces grow;
Where floor of moss infolds the foot,
  Like depths of fallen snow.

Loquacious ravens clack and croak
  Nor hold me in my quest;
The purple grosbeaks perch and sing
  Upon the cedar's crest.

But thou art doomed to shun the day,
  A captive of the shade;
I only catch thy stealthy flight
  Athwart the forest glade.

Thy voice is like a hermit's reed
  That solitude beguiles;
Again 'tis like a silver bell
  Adrift in forest aisles.

Throw off, throw off this masquerade
  And don thy ruddy vest,
And let me find thee, as of old,
  Beside thy orchard nest.

26

A Doubtful Conquest in 1906

by Frederick W. Cook
& Belmore Browne

*For hellish conditions and physical discomforts the
north-pole chase is, compared with Mount McKinley,
tame adventure.   Cook*

*I knew that Dr. Cook had not climbed Mount McKinley . . .
and . . . I knew it in the same way that any New Yorker
would know that no man could walk from the Brooklyn
Bridge to Grant's tomb in ten minutes.   Browne*

Early in the century Cook Inlet became important to another
kind of tourist, the mountain climber who wanted access to the
peaks of interior Alaska. Furthermore, countless gold prospectors and
before them, natives, had seen and reported the existence of a giant
mountain inland, on the right flank of the Susitna River. The peak is
even visible on a clear day from the northern shores of the Inlet. It was
named Mt. McKinley by an unpoetic gold seeker, W. A. Dickey, in
1897. Its identification as the highest mountain in North America was
an irresistible magnet to alpinists looking for unscaled summits.

An alpine assault on "Denali" (another name for the mountain) was
led by Dr. Frederick Cook in 1906. His large party entered the interior

by boat and packtrain, but returned unsuccessful to Cook Inlet, where it disbanded in mid-August. Then Cook, with two packers, decided to reconnoiter the upper Susitna approaches. After a quick journey, he made an astounding announcement which Belmore Browne (a member of the first expedition) was disinclined to believe. (The polar controversy to which Browne refers here, was a later dispute triggered by Cook's claim that he reached the North Pole first.)

Dr. Cook's Story

After a long siege, during which we were compelled to acknowledge several disheartening defeats, we have at last conquered the highest mountain of our continent. In the prolonged expenditure of energy at high pressure this siege of Mount McKinley proved more difficult than most of the arctic projects. We were not days or weeks, but months, in desperate positions, fording icy glacial streams, pushing through thick underbrush, crossing life-sapping marshes and tundras, enduring the tortures of mosquitoes, camping on the top of wind-swept peaks, and being drenched from above and below with frigid waters; in snow-storms, on ice, in gloomy canyons and gulches; on ice cornices and precipices, always with torment and death before us. For danger, hardship, and maddening torture this essay of the great mid-Alaskan peak has been my worst experience. For hellish conditions and physical discomforts the north-pole chase is, compared with Mount McKinley, tame adventure.

Two expeditions were organized in recent years, at a combined cost of twenty-eight thousand dollars, to explore and climb Mount McKinley. An account of the first venture was published in *Harper's Magazine* of February and March of 1894. The last venture was organized in April, 1906.

Many months were previously spent in perfecting an equipment which would be light, and efficient under the severe test of exploring difficult lowlands and climbing high slopes in mid-Alaska, so near the arctic circle. To this end we adapted as far as possible the working equipment of polar explorers.

Our success was very largely due to the extreme simplicity and lightness of our climbing outfit and food. Our aim was to make an independent unit of each man, so that the party could be made up of two or more men as the conditions or our numbers warranted. All men were expected to carry an equal weight in their packs, and that weight was to be made up as far as possible of the entire needs for about two weeks, such as food, clothing, and bedding. The things which differed radically from all other alpine enterprises were a new form of silk tent large enough for three men, weighing but three pounds and requiring no pole; a sleeping-bag which could be converted into a coat or robe, weighing five pounds; and all of the usual climbers' food was discarded for pemmican, which is made of equal quantities of beef tallow and dried beef; also erbswurst, tea, sugar, and biscuits. These biscuits were baked and dried before leaving the timber zone. With our mountain needs thus simplified, I could with one or two trustworthy companions make rapid progress up difficult slopes, over mountainous country which in the usual manner of mountaineering would require a long train of porters and helpers, with the inevitable halts, accidents, and failures.

Belmore Browne's Story

Dr. Cook . . . decided to take Barrill and a new hired man and prospect the upper Susitna River to see if reaching Mount McKinley by that route was feasible. He asked me if I would go up the Matanuska River on the northern slopes of the Chugach Mountains and collect some zoological specimens for him. I told him that if he contemplated exploring the southern foothills of Mount McKinley I would prefer going with him. He answered that he would do no exploring outside of seeing whether or not the water route was practicable and he again urged me to aid him with his game collection. I agreed to help him, and went aboard a small steamer that was lying at Tyonek on her way to the mouth of the Matanuska. . . .

Before leaving Tyonek I invited Dr. Cook aboard to take luncheon with me, and while he was on board or while the boat was at Seldovia he sent the following telegram to a well-known business man of New York City:

"Am preparing for a last, desperate attack on Mount McKinley."

I proceeded up the Matanuska and the Knik rivers and returned after a short and successful hunt to Seldovia. . . .

At this time we heard the rumour that Dr. Cook and Barrill had reached the top of Mount McKinley. We knew the character of country that guarded the southern face of the big mountain, we had travelled in that country, and we knew the time that Dr. Cook had been absent was too short to allow of his even reaching the mountain. We therefore denied the rumour. At last the Doctor and Barrill joined us and to my surprise Dr. Cook confirmed the rumour. After a word with Dr. Cook I called Barrill aside, and we walked up the Seldovia beach. Barrill and I had been through some hard times together. I liked Barrill and I knew that he was fond of me for we were tied by the strong bond of having suffered together. As soon as we were alone I turned to him and asked him what he knew about Mount McKinley, and after a moment's hesitation he answered: "I can tell you all about the big peaks just south of the mountain, but if you want to know about Mount McKinley go and ask Cook." I had felt all along that Barrill would tell me the truth, and after his statement I kept the knowledge to myself. . . .

I now found myself in an embarrassing position. I knew that Dr. Cook had not climbed Mount McKinley. Barrill had told me so and in addition I knew it in the same way that any New Yorker would know that no man could walk from the Brooklyn Bridge to Grant's tomb in ten minutes.

This knowledge, however, did not constitute proof, and I knew that before I could make the public believe the truth I should have to collect some facts. I wrote immediately on my return to Professor Parker telling him my opinions and knowledge concerning the climb, and I received a reply from him saying that he believed me implicitly and that the climb, under the existing conditions, was impossible.

I returned to New York as soon as possible and both Professor Parker and I stated our convictions to members of the American Geographical Society and the Explorers' Club.

Many of these men were warm friends of Doctor Cook. We, however, knew the question was above partisanship, and were willing to give Doctor Cook every chance to clear himself. . . .

Before his book was published, however, Dr. Cook sailed *secretly* to the North. Both Professor Parker and myself were present at the gathering of the Explorers' Club when his farewell telegram was read. It was rather significant in view of the fact that he had many good friends in the club that no applause or signs of enthusiasm followed the reading of his message.

After the appearance of Dr. Cook's book Professor Parker and I found ourselves in possession of irrefutable proof that Dr. Cook had made countless misstatements in his description of the route he followed to the mountain, and the equipment he used. Many of the misstatements we knew to be downright falsehoods. We were influenced, however, by our own ideas of fair play as well as the suggestions of our friends, and we refrained from publishing anything derogatory to the Doctor's character while he was absent, and unable to defend himself. . . .

The reader will remember the excitement of Dr. Cook's return and the Polar controversy that followed, and I will skip all the public details of this period of Dr. Cook's notoriety.

In looking back on that remarkable controversy I am still filled with astonishment at the incredible amount of vindictive and personal spite that was shown by the partisans of Doctor Cook. Men who had never seen an ice-axe or a sled-dog wrote us reams of warped exploring details and accused us of untold crimes because we had dared to question Cook's honesty.

I was visiting Professor Parker at that time and scarcely a day went by when we did not receive abusive anonymous letters. In the face of this blind public partisanship, we realised that we would need more than documentary and circumstantial evidence to convict Doctor Cook irrevocably. The Polar controversy had put an entirely new light on our claims against Cook.

27

The Government Railroad & Anchorage in 1917

by Theodore Pilger

*The sale of liquor is unlawful, but liberal allowances
are made for private use, and it is a very wet "dry" town.*

A few years after the Cook episode, mountain climbers could
approach close to McKinley with ease (if not always in perfect
comfort) aboard the Alaska Railroad, completed in 1923. It was a
federal railroad constructed to tap the territory's natural resources,
after private railroad enterprises failed to penetrate the interior.
Newcomers to the State's largest city may forget that Anchorage was
founded by the government railroad, which remained the town's major
basic industry until the coming of World War II and a large military
establishment. The townsite was even surveyed by federal engineers
and lots were sold at government auctions; during eight days in July
1915, 655 lots were sold for an average price of $230 each. The following
article, describing the railroad and Anchorage two years later, is from
the *Mining and Scientific Press.*

The first serious agitation for a government-owned and government-operated railroad started in 1911, during the Taft administration, while Walter L. Fisher was Secretary of the Interior. He visited Alaska, and recommended that the coal-lands be leased, also that the Bering River and Matanuska Valley coals be tested by the Navy Department, and that a Government railroad be built from Seward to the Matanuska coalfield, should that coal prove satisfactory. In 1912, a commission, known as the Taft Commission, having examined all the feasible routes, recommended that the Government should build from the station of Chitina on the Copper River & Northwestern railroad to the town of Fairbanks in the interior.

With the Wilson administration came Franklin K. Lane as Secretary of the Interior. Although he has never visited Alaska, he has taken a keen interest in the development of the territory. He personally pushed the Railroad Act, and the Coal Lands Leasing Act, both of which were passed in 1914. By the Railroad Act, the President of the United States is restricted to cause to be built not more than 1000 miles of railroad, and to expend not to exceed $35,000,000 thereon. President Wilson created the Alaska Engineering Commission, composed of W. C. Edes, chairman, Frederick Mears, and Thomas Riggs, Jr., members. . . .

This commission first made preliminary surveys of various proposed lines, and finally recommended the Seward-Broad

Pass-Fairbanks route, which runs from Seward on the west shore of Resurrection bay, northward through the Kenai peninsula, thence westward along the north shore of Turnagain Arm, along the east shore of Knik Arm, across the Knik and Matanuska rivers, in a north-westerly direction through the Susitna valley, across Broad Pass, down the Nenana river, and up Gold stream to Fairbanks. It also recommended the route of a branch line, designated from a point two miles north from where the main line crosses the Matanuska river, running thence in an easterly direction into the Matanuska coalfield.

These recommendations having been adopted, the Commission then purchased the 71 miles of [existing private] railroad from Seward to Kern creek for $1,500,000, although over $4,000,000 had been expended on this railroad by the original owners; and the 40 miles of narrow-gauge railroad known as the Tanana Valley Railroad was also purchased at a later date for the sum of $300,000. This bit of railroad goes north from Fairbanks and acts as a feeder to the main line. The reasons for the choice of the Seward-Fairbanks route by the Alaska Engineering Commission was that the railroad could be constructed with the least expense, as there were no great obstacles to overcome, and it was believed that this route would aid the development of the greatest amount of resources with benefit to the greatest number of people. . . .

Beginning at Seward, which has an open harbor the year round, on Resurrection bay, the railroad passes near the placer mines on the Kenai river. There are several quartz mines at various points on the railroad side of the Kenai peninsula, and fairly well-developed placer and lode claims above Sunrise and Hope, two camps on the same peninsula. Passing near placers on Glacier creek, the railroad runs through the agricultural lands around the town of Anchorage that open out into the broad valleys of the Matanuska and Susitna rivers. On the upper Matanuska branch are the seams that, it is hoped, will develop into producers of Pacific Coast coal. The centre of this coal district is the new railroad town of Chickaloon.

* * *

The most difficult [construction] work has been in rock for about 30 miles along the north side of Turnagain Arm. Here the cost will be as much as $100,000 per mile for the grading and bridging alone. This should be completed by the spring of 1918, and the line completed through from Seward early in the summer. Some difficulty is being experienced in crossing the large terminal moraine below Spencer glacier on the Kenai peninsula, but it is not regarded as serious. The Commission has purchased a large amount of equipment, which it will have on its hands when this road is completed, and it is believed that it will be the policy of the Government to build railroad-feeders to the main line from both the east and the west to furnish sufficient tonnage to render the road profitable. No part of the railroad is expected to be endangered by snow-slides, although it is probable that there will be some trouble from the deep snows in the Susitna valley and between Turnagain Arm and Seward. Many snow-sheds will undoubtedly have to be built.

* * *

The entire system has been divided into the Anchorage, Fairbanks, and Seward divisions, which employ collectively about 4500 men. Of this number, 2900 are employed on the Anchorage division, about 900 on the Seward division, and about 700 on the Fairbanks division. Seward is considered the terminal of the railroad, and Anchorage the terminal of the Anchorage division, which is, however, the most important division of the three. At Anchorage the Government will attempt to solve the difficulties connected with the maintaining of an open harbor on upper Cook's Inlet, by dredging and building a large cribbed stone wharf. Here will be built the bunkers to receive the Matanuska coal. The water of Knik Arm, at Anchorage is, of course, salt, and consequently does not freeze at the prevailing temperature, which has never exceeded -38°. The difficulty at Anchorage is the fact that large rivers and creeks bring with them blocks of ice, up to 40 ft. diam., and 4 ft. or more thick, which collect in Knik Arm above a constricted opening opposite Campbell Point. This ice settles on the mud flats at low tide, and freezes to the ground. On the return of the tide, the blocks of ice are lifted and carry with them considerable earth. This, repeated time after time, builds up combined ice and mud blocks that are a great menace to vessels lying at anchor. The tidal difference ranges from 36 to 42 ft., and this water at ebb and flow attains a velocity up to 7 knots per hour. It is the difficulty of withstanding the pressure of these blocks of mud-ice, traveling at such a velocity, that prevents uninterrupted shipping from Anchorage.

To overcome this the Commission has determined to build a wharf 80 ft. high, 1000 ft. long, which will give 6 fathoms at low water, and will allow for a 42-ft. rise in the tide. This wharf will be built in the re-entrant angle of a crescent shore-line, about 3/4 mile north from the mouth of Ship creek. . . . Upon the completion of this plan the Commission is certain that vessels will be able to enter Knik Arm on flow tide, discharge, load cargoes, and pass out on ebb tide on any day of the year. It is to be noted that whereas it is likely that most of the freight from the interior will be transferred to vessels at the wharf, which will save a 115-mile haul from Anchorage to Seward over two mountain passes, one 700 ft., the other 1100 ft. high, most of the passengers will probably go over the railroad from one of these points to the other, taking a four-hour trip by railroad in preference to a 20-hour trip by boat around the Kenai peninsula in stormy weather. In addition to the wharf built for use by ocean-going vessels, it is planned by the Commission to dredge for a small wharf nearer to the town of Anchorage, to accommodate the "mosquito fleet" on Cook's Inlet. The new harbor improvements are expected to be sufficiently completed to handle traffic by the fall of 1918.

* * *

There is some loose talk of making either Anchorage or Seward the capital of Alaska, and there is a great likelihood of the territory tributary to Anchorage being formed into another judicial district, which would make the fifth. The President has authority to either operate or lease the railroad. During the summer of 1917 the railroad was short between 500 and 1000 men, but in November there is an over-supply until work is resumed in April. . . .

Anchorage, on the level bench at the base of the . . . mountains, and at the mouth of Ship creek, is a city with a population of between 6000 and 7000. It is only a little over two years old. One of its banks, which started with a capitalization of $25,000, now has deposits of over $750,000. It is a division point and the second ocean port for the Government railroad. It is certain to be the principal coal-freight terminal for nine months of the year, if not for twelve. The summers are mild and the winters are not severe; being farther back from the Pacific the average temperature is a few degrees lower, and the rain and snow-fall less than at Seward. The summer days never end. Only twilight intervenes between two warm mellow days, but the days of winter are correspondingly brief. It does not resemble any typical Alaskan town, and neither is it like a boom town of a new mining district in the States. The Government has a large and well-appointed hospital, and buildings for all the departments of the railroad's operations. There is a large post-office, a telephone, telegraph, and electric-light office, a fine Masonic temple, several churches, lodge quarters, Y.M.C.A., and club-rooms. It has the largest labor temple in Alaska, a good school, well graded streets, the thoroughfares having concrete and the side streets board walks. The sale of liquor is unlawful, but liberal allowances are made for private use, and it is a very wet "dry" town. January 1918 will change this, however, for then all Alaska will come under prohibition. The town boasts a large number of pretty and substantial homes, including those built by the Government for its employees, having electric lights and modern sewerage. The surrounding country is remarkably beautiful. In the distance can be seen at all times the splendid stretch of the Alaskan range, and on clear days Mt. McKinley rears its snow-crowned head against the blue, 20,300 ft. high and 175 miles distant.

28

Grubbing in the Matanuska Valley, 1915-1917

by M. D. Snodgrass

*Methods of clearing the land at present are various and
crude: grubbing with mattock and shovel; cutting some
of the roots and lining with rope through a lead block;
pulling stumps with homemade stump pullers, and
burning during the dry seasons.*

The railroad's arrival renewed hopes for the agricultural
development of Alaska. The common American expectation was
that railroads would open to cultivation new land and provide access to
markets for agricultural products. Near Cook Inlet, to a limited degree,
that was true; railroad construction workers were the market, and the
Matanuska Valley, at the head of Knik Arm, was already the scene of
homesteading on a large scale and farming on a small scale. But before
the Jeffersonian dream could be realized in Alaska, some back-breaking
work was necessary. In 1917, M. D. Snodgrass of the U.S. Department
of Agriculture station at Kodiak, outlined in print some of the real
problems and the optimistic possibilities.

*T*he real problem confronting the new settlers is in clearing the land. The greater portion of land in the Matanuska Valley suitable for cultivation is covered with timber, consisting of spruce, pine, birch, cottonwood, quaking aspen, and alder. The timber ranges from 6 to 24 inches in diameter, with from 200 to 300 trees per acre. The larger trees are found among the cottonwood which grows along the creek bottoms. Groves of birch intermingled with spruce grow on the bench land and low hills, while the spruce with a little hemlock is to be found on the steeper hillsides. Ninety per cent of the timber of the region is less than 12 inches in diameter.

Methods of clearing the land at present are various and crude; grubbing with mattock and shovel; cutting some of the roots and lining with rope through a lead block; pulling stumps with homemade stump pullers, and burning during the dry seasons. Slashing the timber and piling and burning gives fair results where the stump puller is available for pulling the stumps after the burning. The most popular method is to get a "ground burn," which is sometimes possible during the month of June. In such cases, the fire burns the moss and fallen timber and often the roots of the standing timber. Many of the trees fall and burn at the time, but most of them fall later, and afford opportunity for a subsequent burning the next season. The roots of the trees are usually very shallow and are bared by the burning. After a second burning the charred timber left on the ground is piled and burned.

The burning in the moss sometimes runs for five to six weeks, but does not travel more than a few feet a day. . . .

The soil is left loose and fine where a good ground burn has been secured, is easily worked, retains moisture well, and produces well the first year. Where it is impossible to get a good burn, there is considerable moss and vegetation to contend with. This must be raked together in piles, dried and burned, or hauled off the land before cultivation. The burning on the land is beneficial to the soil, and should be resorted to as a general practice. The depth of the soil on the bench lands and low hill lands generally ranges from 1 to 5 feet of volcanic ash covered with a good dark loam of various depths, overlying glacial gravel deposits, while the soil of the creek and river bottoms is largely of silt deposits. The river bottom lands are not very productive, as the soil is too new, yet there are many small areas of this land that produce considerable grass for hay and pasture.

Crops grown in the Matanuska country during the last few years prove beyond a doubt that great possibilities in agriculture are to be found there. Barley, oats, rye, potatoes, cabbage, turnips, ruta-bagas, carrots, tomatoes, cauliflower, beets, and also most all of the common garden vegetables have been grown successfully. Yields of potatoes as high as 12 tons per acre are reported by the settlers. The potato matures and equals in quality the best grown in the States. The hillside lands are especially suited to potato culture, while the terrace or bench lands are excellent for root crops, vegetable gardening, and grain crops. Native hay is confined to small areas, but pasturage is to be found to a limited extent throughout the timberlands. On an average from 3 to 5 acres of timberland will be required for the pasturing of a horse or cow for 5 months in the year. Along the small creeks the pasturage is much better, and small natural parks afford some hay. Tame grasses and also alsike clover grow readily where seeded in burned-over areas. White clover does well where given a chance to grow. Natural meadows and good pasture lands are to be found near and upon the foothills. General stock raising will of necessity be limited to these areas, but excellent opportunities for the establishing of dairy farms with tame-grass pastures are to be found throughout this region.

Wild fruits are abundant in this region, consisting of currants (both red and black), blueberries, salmonberries, raspberries, gooseberries, cranberries, and a number of other edible sorts. The strawberries so common on the coast of southeastern Alaska are not found here, but wherever planted they grow well. Practically all the cultivated varieties of berries can be grown with profit.

Settlement of the surveyed lands along the Matanuska River has been rapid this season. Practically all the agricultural land in this vicinity was taken by July 1, 1915. Much of the surveyed land lying to the west of the Matanuska Valley, to the north of Knik Arm, and ranging northwest to the Little Susitna has been taken up, and homesteaders are still going into that region. It is practically assured that all the desirable agricultural land will be settled upon as rapidly as the Government railroad penetrates the region. Transportation facilities are the prime factors in the development of this entire region. Wherever transportation by water has been possible the new settlers have pushed ahead into the wilderness and have already begun their clearings and built their homes. In many instances the entire outfits, home furnishing and machinery, have been brought in on pack horses from 5 to 15 miles. Log cabins are to be found springing up in the center of many small clearings, and the settlers are hard at work clearing more ground, planting, hoeing, and building. A number of comfortable log houses and barns are to be found, and a few herds of dairy cows are already taking their place in the new settlements. Hogs and chickens are also finding their places in the new order of things.

The settlers are of the hardy pioneer class, largely of the Scandinavian nationality, who have come into the country with the determination and grit so characteristic of that people. They make use of the building materials at hand, hew the logs, whipsaw enough lumber for finishing and flooring, and sometimes for roofing their cabins. The employment of birch bark for roofing material is in evidence.

The cutting and building of trails and roads has begun, and the country is far more accessible to-day than two years ago. The building of roads throughout this country is the one great need at present. The building of Government roads and trails as feeders to the railroad will materially aid and hasten the agricultural development. During the winter months the settlers work on the trails leading to their homesteads from the established trails, or on the wagon road between Knik and Willow Creek Mines. The trails are usually wide enough to accommodate a single horse, double-end sled, which affords a good temporary method of transportation of freight from tidewater to the remote settlements. The trails will gradually give way to wagon roads, which can readily be built through the greater part of this region at a moderate cost, most of which will be [for] the removal of the timber. Gravels are available for road work through the low hills and bench lands. But few tundra areas are encountered in the region.

Climatic conditions are quite favorable to general farming. The winters are rather long, but are even in temperature and not severe. The summers are warm, and favorable growing weather can be expected from May 1 to September 1. The long hours of sunshine during the summer time go far to make up for the seemingly short season. . . .

Considerable land suitable for farming is to be found within the National Forest about Anchorage, but the depth of the soil is not so great, and the soil is more acid than that found along the Matanuska Valley, the temperature is not so high, and the frosts are reported a little earlier in the fall than in the Matanuska Valley. Within the National Forest homesteads not exceeding 160 acres in area may be secured where the land is chiefly valuable for farming. Each tract is examined by the Department of Agriculture before it is opened to filing or settlement is allowed. . . .

The surveying and opening of the Susitna Valley will afford 10,000 or 12,000 homesteads of 160 acres each.

This country will bear close inspection by those seeking a homestead and is well worth the time and cost of a tour of inspection. The development must come through those who are willing and able to do hard work, but the establishment of many comfortable homes may reasonably be expected within a few years.

29

A Petroleum Seepage near Anchorage, 1921

by Alfred Hulse Brooks

*. . . the presence of oil in this region, except for the small
seepage described. . . can be proved only by drilling . . .
[and] all drilling . . . must be classed as wildcatting.*

A false indicator of Anchorage's immediate future was contained
in the 1921 report of Alfred Hulse Brooks, geologist and
explorer. He reported an oil seepage within what is now Greater
Anchorage. Wealth from the petroleum industry's corporate
bureaucracy headquartered in Anchorage came much later to the town,
but who knows what fluid black gold has been lurking beneath the
backyard of the Anchorage suburbanite?

*P*rior to 1921 no evidence of petroleum near Anchorage had been found. Some shallow drilling had been done, but it did not reach the hard rock, and the character of the nearest exposed formations gave no encouragement to the hope of finding oil at greater depths. In July, 1921, however, a small petroleum seepage was found in sec. 24, T. 23, R. 3, about a mile southwest of the town of Anchorage. This locality was visited in August, and oil seeping from a gravel bank on top of a clay layer at about sea level was found. The seepage was estimated to yield about 2 fluid ounces a day. Its location precluded the possibility of its being due to an accidental leakage from an oil tank.

* * *

There is no positive evidence of the source of the petroleum of this seepage. The surface of the region for several miles is mantled with a cover of gravel and sand, probably at least 300 feet thick. Soft sandstones containing a little lignitic coal occur on the shores of Knik Arm, not far from the seepages. So far as known these beds are only gently tilted. Even if oil might be distilled from the vegetable remains in these beds, the fact that the formation is nearly unaltered except for slight cementation of sandstone seems to preclude the idea that the physical conditions have been favorable to distillation. Moreover, the same Tertiary lignite-bearing beds occur in large areas both north and south of this locality. These beds have been examined in considerable detail, but nowhere have they revealed any evidence that they contain petroleum, and they can with confidence be excluded as a possible source of this oil. This seepage occurs near the eastern margin of the great Susitna lowland, which covers over 1,500 square miles and is filled with silts, sands, and gravels to an unknown but probably great depth. These delta deposits undoubtedly contain some vegetable remains and possibly some animal remains. It is not impossible that such deposits might afford favorable conditions for the formation of petroleum, but such an explanation of the facts in hand is a mere speculation. Moreover, the unconsolidated silts, sands, and gravels certainly do not afford favorable conditions for the formation of oil pools.

With regard to a possible hard-rock source for this oil the available facts obtainable from outcrops are all negative. The gravel bench from which the oil emerges stretches eastward for 7 miles to the base of the mountains, mantling all rock exposures. In the mountains the formations consist of closely folded and faulted altered sediments and igneous rocks, possibly of Mesozoic age, but entirely unfavorable to the presence of petroleum and so much altered and disturbed as to preclude the possibility that they contain oil pools.

The outcropping bedrock in the vicinity of Anchorage therefore affords no clue to the source of the seepage oil. The great lowland described is occupied almost entirely by alluvial deposits, the only bedrock being a few outcrops of the Tertiary lignite-bearing beds. Neither of these formations is a promising source of petroleum. The formations in the highland bounding this alluvium-covered lowland are not believed to be oil bearing, yet this lowland tract may itself contain oil-bearing rocks. The nearest known oil-bearing rocks are those of Iniskin Bay, 150 miles to the south, which are of Jurassic age. The extension of the strike of these distant formations would carry them into the lowland region near the eastern margin of which the Anchorage seepage is situated. If the Anchorage seepage is derived from such buried oil-bearing rocks, a careful search in the lowland region should lead to the discovery of other seepages, if they have not already been found.

Evidently, therefore, the presence of oil in this region, except for the small seepage described or others that may be found, can be proved only by drilling. In the absence of bedrock exposures, geologic examinations are of little or no value. The fact that the region is readily accessible by steamer, railroad, and wagon road will make it far less expensive to drill than other parts of Alaska. It should be added, however, that in the absence of any clue to the structure and any knowledge of the depth of the oil-bearing formations, even if they are present, all drilling in this region must be classed as wildcatting.

30

A New Deal for Agriculture (1952)

by Hugh A. Johnson

*Dairying appears to be the climax type of farm organization
in the Matanuska Valley with a few specialized potato
and truck farms interspersed throughout.*

With the railroad in operation, Anchorage settled back to
enjoy what was left of the Roaring Twenties, and then
muddled quietly through the Great Depression. President Franklin
Roosevelt's New Deal brought a measure of attention and a dollop of
dollars to the region in 1935, when the Federal Emergency Relief
Administration resettled unemployed, northern middle-westerners in
the Matanuska Valley. After 1939 the farm colony sold its products to
the people who constructed and staffed the new military bases. The
next document describes the situation at Matanuska by 1952. Since
then, the farm sector has remained small, but the hope that Alaska will
one day support a large and prosperous agricultural industry is still
alive. In 1964, the U.S. Department of Agriculture spent
approximately $7,500,000 in Alaska, where there were just under 400
farms—an indirect subsidy averaging $19,000 per farm. The
expenditure was $2,000,000 more than the value of the agricultural
product.

*D*ue to the rapid expansion of both the Anchorage metropolitan area and the nearby military installations, there are considered to be no agricultural lands from Turnagain Arm up the east side of Cook Inlet to the Knik River. North of the Knik River at the head of Cook Inlet lies the Matanuska Valley, home of the famous Matanuska Colony, and the Susitna Valley lies to the west. . . .

There were 117 families having a total of over 1,000 acres cleared in the Matanuska Valley prior to 1935 and the advent of the Colony. Old reports show that a considerable tonnage of potatoes was harvested during the railroad construction period. As soon as the railroad was completed, however, no market could be found for potatoes and other vegetables.

For several years the Alaska Railroad operated a small creamery at Curry. Later it was moved to the Matanuska Experiment

Station. These steps laid the groundwork for the Matanuska Valley Farmers Cooperating Association's creamery and dairy plant which in 1951-1952 did a gross business of $1,542,000.

Agricultural development of this area was slow until the outbreak of World War II even with the financial and physical aid of the Matanuska Colony. Proponents of the Colony believed that small, subsistence type farms were desirable in Alaska; their plans and programs called for 40-acre tracts with the operators working away from the farm to earn the cash necessary for living. Many settlers apparently had different ideas. Some left their 40-acre tracts. Others held on and added to their original holdings whenever adjacent lands became available. Specialized farming is developing as rapidly as land can be cleared for it.

While average holdings of cleared land were small, settlers had no alternative but to farm intensively, producing chiefly truck crops and potatoes. These required large amounts of hand labor and returned a large income per acre. The colonization land-clearing program was completed in 1948 and land clearing since that time has been done by private contract.

Between 600 and 700 acres per year have been cleared in this area during each of the years 1949-52. Consequently, about 75 farms now have sufficient cleared land to allow specialized full-time farming. About 60 of these are commercial dairy farms having an average of 75 acres of cropland and 15 dairy cows. The other 15 farms grow potatoes or vegetables having an average of about 40 acres in crops. Approximately 200 additional families have smaller acreages in production and still depend on non-farm income to supplement their potato and truck crop enterprises. Some 15 poultry flocks of between 150 and 1,200 birds are located in the area. Most of them are supplemental enterprises on dairy or truck farms.

Dairying appears to be the climax type of farm organization in the Matanuska Valley with a few specialized potato and truck farms interspersed throughout. Because winter winds cause severe soil erosion over much of this section, winter ground cover must be provided. Grass pastures, meadows and grain stubble are necessary for soil protection in most farm plans.

In the eastern and central portions of the Matanuska Valley, virtually all tillable land is in private ownership. All the good land is taken. Nearly all farm holdings include uncleared portions which will be cleared eventually for crop production. Few farms now are of optimum size for efficient field management. Farm transfers occur fairly frequently and opportunities are good for buying developed or partially developed tracts in the Matanuska Valley proper.

Farms in the western Matanuska Valley and the lower Susitna Valley are scattered, partly because shallow soils limit profitable land use to a livestock economy, partly because transportation is unavailable and partly due to the recency of homesteading in the area. About 2½ townships in this area were opened to homesteading in August 1947. Most veterans who acquired tracts lacked capital and experience to develop operating units. Many of these tracts now are in absentee ownership.

31

The
Good Friday Quake
of 1964

by Saul Pett & Jules Loh

*. . . across 600 miles of mountains and towns and spruce
forests and icy streams and secluded coves and great
expanses of snow broken only by animal tracks the earth
strained and groaned and shook.*

In 1964, after statehood had come to Alaska and after military
construction had begun to taper off, Mother Nature took
southcentral Alaska by the lapels and gave it a thorough shaking. The
great earthquake of that year was one of the most severe in the history
of seismology. The shattering event provided those Alaskans who
survived with a common experience in terror and cooperation.

193

*T*hat afternoon Louis Beaty noticed something strange. His 200 head of cattle were grazing quietly at his ranch on Narrow Cape, a lovely finger of land washed by the Gulf of Alaska, about 50 miles southeast of Kodiak on the Gulf of Kodiak.

About three o'clock that afternoon, the cattle turned and began to move away from their low-lying grazing land to higher ground. They had never done this before so early in the day.

Louis Beaty frowned. The sky was sunny and blue. The mountains behind him stood serenely in their skirts of new snow. The wind blowing in from the turquoise sea was gentle.

Beaty vaguely sensed that the cattle had sensed something. But what?

What, indeed? The mood of Alaska on this Good Friday, March 27, 1964, was benign. Spring was coming, the temperature was rising. People were already betting on when the ice would break up in the rivers. Even in this age of flight, the ice breakup remains symbolic to Alaskans. The winter feeling of isolation was about to yield to the friendliness of spring, like opening a window onto "the outside," onto the rest of the United States.

Down deep under the earth's crust, more than 50 miles down, in an eternal darkness without season, it is thought that a huge river of slowly swirling, boiling pitch-like substance rings the great iron core of the earth. Just what was happening down there on this Good Friday no man on earth could say with certainty and cows make unreliable seismologists. One theory is that this huge river by its constant and opposing currents wears and strains the earth's crust. Where the crust is weak, it may crack. Alaska is known to lie on a relative weak layer of crust.

At her tidy frame home in Anchorage, Joan Groom couldn't have cared less about the mysterious forces grinding and straining the earth beneath. Of more immediate concern were the visible forces that could at any moment wreck her living room and nervous system.

The children, at last, were in their places; the pink cake with its cover of coconut was on the table, her daughter Claudia had made her wish and was now ready to blow out the four pink candles. Ten young critics, four of them her brothers and sisters, were yelling she couldn't do it in one puff.

Downtown, Harry Groom, a photographer, was starting home. Recalling his daughter's party, he decided on one quick fortification against the inevitable chaos. He pulled up at the "Highland Fling," where they sell two drinks for the price of one between 5 and 6 o'clock, went inside and ordered bourbon.

Out in the quiet suburb called "Turnagain," a well-birched subdivision of ranch and split level houses, Esther McCreedy was finishing a ham with brown sugar and pineapple rings. Her husband was due home for supper in about 20 minutes.

Far to the south, 250 miles from Claudia Groom's birthday party and 50 miles northwest of Louis Beaty's curiously acting cattle, Bill Cuthbert, a leathery and grizzled fisherman, was sitting down to supper in the galley of his 86-foot scow, the *Selief*. The boat was tied to its slip in Kodiak Harbor, a picturesque horseshoe at the foot of the mountains. In the hold were $3,000 worth of Alaska king crabs, ready to be unloaded next morning at the cannery.

Atop the hill above the harbor, in the sanctuary of St. James the Fisherman Episcopal Church, carpenter Louis Horn was hanging a new cross above the alter. It was now 5:20 p.m. Horn selected two small eye bolts to suspend the heavy cross from the ceiling.

"Do you think these will hold it, Louis?" asked the Rev. Donald Bullock.

"Sure, Father."

"What if we have an earthquake," the father chuckled.

"Even in an earthquake," laughed the carpenter.

By Alaska standards, it was warm, about 35 degrees in Kodiak and Anchorage and the infrequent towns and remote villages in between. But 1,500 miles down the rim of the great Pacific basin, at Newport, Oregon, it was much warmer and Monte and Rita McKenzie and their four children had gone to the shore on a camping trip.

They found a cozy spot for the night, a driftwood shelter on the beach north of Newport. The sea glowed in the light of a full moon. The McKenzie family, clustered tightly together, soon fell asleep. After seven months, the pain of their nine-year-old daughter's death had begun to ebb.

And in the serenity that bathed the moonlit beach in Oregon, the gentle harbor in Kodiak and the quiet going home time in Anchorage, the earth crust under Alaska could no longer endure the strain of the inexorable forces below. It let go at 5:36 p.m., Anchorage time.

And across more than 600 miles of mountains and towns and spruce forests and icy streams and secluded coves and great expanses of snow broken only by animal tracks the earth strained and groaned and shook.

And in untold hundreds of places it cracked open and in scores of places it buckled and toppled buildings and swayed trees and poles in wild dizzy arcs and heaved up pavement and snapped bridges and sheared avalanches of snow and dirt and stone from mountain tops and out in the sea it raised a mighty wave.

In Anchorage, Joan Groom's house quivered, then shook with increasing force. The chimney crashed onto the roof and the birthday cake smashed on the floor. Screaming with fright, the children toppled over in their chairs. Joan Groom lost her balance and pitched to the floor in a litter of flying books and glass and overturned furniture.

Again and again the house shook, sometimes gently, sometimes violently. Then suddenly it ended. Somehow no one was injured.

197

White with terror, Joan Groom began to sing a song the children had memorized. Slowly, one by one, they stopped crying and began singing:

"The little book shelf
"Is wiggling itself
"And the books are falling down.
"The fairy tales and fables
"Are tumbling over chairs and tables.
"Mother Goose is running loose,
"She is marching into town."

At the Highland Fling, Harry Groom felt the first tremor and smiled.

"Oh," he said flippantly, "another earthquake." Others at the bar smiled. After many years of gentle tremors and no real quake, Alaskans had come to regard the subject with nonchalance.

But this tremor refused to stop, and the bar fell quiet and then the whole room rocked with new force. Bottles pitched to the floor, glasses smashed, women screamed. People tried to rush to the door but the floor was billowing like insane jello and they fell and they crawled. Harry Groom finally made it to the street, still holding, for no reason he remembered, the two-for-one glasses, unbroken. Like husbands everywhere in town, he was trying to get home to his family.

Outside, on Fourth Avenue, the pavement was billowing and people were falling and cars were bouncing and one whole block of stores sank—just sank—20 feet into a huge crack of the convulsed earth. The marquee of the Denali Movie Theater, which was to open in a half hour for the evening show, sank to the level of the sidewalk.

A block away, the five-story J. C. Penney building swayed out over the street, swayed back and then one end sank in a roar of crumbling masonry and glass. Elsewhere, a new six-story apartment, not yet occupied, collapsed in thunder and in many places earth fissures snaked right through living rooms.

At the 14-story Mt. McKinley Apartments, one of Anchorage's two tallest buildings, Delphine Haley was riding the elevator near the eighth floor. The elevator quivered and stopped. Then it began bouncing up and down, up and down, and Delphine Haley screamed in terror. The whole world, it seemed to her, was screaming.

The elevator stopped bouncing momentarily between floors and she squeezed through a 10-inch opening in the doors and climbed to the floor above. She made her way to the stairwell and in the darkness, in the incredible shaking and swaying, she became hysterical. Crying, she pitched herself headlong down each flight, crawled across the landing, and pitching and crawling finally made her way to the ground floor and out. She looked back and saw others crawling groggily out of the building. Up the entire face of the structure the apartment was scarred by a series of zig-zagging cracks.

When Esther McCreedy's ham pitched from the stove she knew it was no ordinary tremor and hurried out. Near the door she was thrown down by a violent new shudder. And just outside the door, she turned and watched her home sink "as if in slow motion" up to roof level in a huge crevasse.

Beyond, where 100 homes had stood, she saw an eerie expanse of ruin. The bluffs overlooking Cook Inlet had fallen away, 200 yards inland, taking with it houses snapped in two and three pieces into deep gorges. The area looked like a vast brown sea of motionless waves, peaked with pieces of homes and snapped trees. Esther McCreedy wept.

And suddenly it was over—some say after 90 seconds, others after five full minutes—and now all of Anchorage, it seems, was arrested in an unfamiliar, overwhelmingly complete silence.

And from far out in the agitated ocean came the wave rushing toward the shaken land. As the depth grew shallower, the wave grew higher. Where it hit the land in broad open areas it looked like a broad, suddenly rising tide. Where it had to pass through a narrow passage, as it did at Seward, 130 miles south of Anchorage, it gathered momentum and force and raced forward like a wall of water.

Far away in Oregon waves swept in on the McKenzie family asleep on the beach. The parents escaped but their four young children were swept to their deaths in the sea.

On it rushed toward Seward, a town of 1,900 which in eight days was to celebrate its selection as an "All American City" because of its economic self-improvement. It was now 5:44, eight minutes after the quake hit Seward, and a wall of water 40 feet high rushed through the narrow mountainous passage of Resurrection Bay. It smashed over the new town port, ripped boats loose from the dock,

199

sent everything in its path tumbling forward, including a 60-ton locomotive which ended up six blocks away.

In seconds, it seemed, Seward was left a wasteland of destroyed houses and broken railroad cars all looking like toys angrily smashed by a wanton child. The big fuel tanks near the dock tumbled in the onslaught and oil spread across the waters. Suddenly, the water took fire and a wave of flame rushed toward the head of the bay.

Ahead of the flames, small boats raced for the shore and many, riding the crest of the tidal wave, sailed over trees 30 feet high and ended up on a pasture on the inland side of the woods.

In town, Doug McRae and his family, including a three-week-old baby, climbed a garage roof and from there stepped across to a house roof. The wave hit, carrying off the garage and part of the house. The roof floated off with the McRaes on it and after about 15 minutes lodged against four tall trees.

There the McRaes shivered for hours. They ripped open a hole in the roof, tore out insulation and wrapped themselves in it. The moon was out and they could see dogs floating by and saw their own car tumble past. To them, it seemed that the whole town was afire. Finally, the water and fire receded and the McRaes were rescued without serious injury.

Far to the southwest, on Kodiak Island, the quake shook Louis Beaty's ranch house but he and his clairvoyant cattle were safe on high ground. At the narrow head of Shearwater Bay, the great quake opened long fissures, the bay rushed in, the ground snapped shut and towering geysers shot skyward.

At the town of Kodiak, the quake was less spectacular. It shook houses, tumbled dishes, but somehow Father Bullock's cross clung to the wall. Up in the hills, a later inspection of tracks showed, the quake shook many Kodiak brown bears out of their winter hibernation two weeks early and sent them in huge jumps down toward the shore. For at least two weeks now they must wander without normal food supplies.

Out in the harbor, Skipper Bill Cuthbert cursed. He was sure some drunken sailor had bumped into his boat. Cuthbert stormed out on deck and saw masts waving madly all over the bay. He realized at once it was an earthquake and turned on his radio to the emergency marine band. Few Alaskan seamen need to be told that quakes make waves.

State Trooper Don Church, back in Kodiak only a half hour after a 22-day tour of his district—the entire Aleutian Chain where he knows every village and nomadic family—rushed to the police station to sound the alarm over the marine radio: Expect a tidal wave; get to high ground.

But Bill Cuthbert couldn't; he had a lame engine. With no choice, with his boat tied to the dock, he went to the galley and waited. The first wave came at 6:47 p.m.—gently, a gradual swell followed by a gradual ebb.

It was now dark and the townspeople who had scampered up the hills with flashlights now looked like fireflies. The second wave hit with a roar and in an instant every piling, every anchor, every line, every pier, snapped and broke and the harbor became a dizzy whirlpool.

Cuthbert dashed to the wheelhouse while his two crewmen clung to the rail. They heard a man in a small boat crying for help. They tried to throw him a line but couldn't. They saw his small boat carried off crazily in a wild maelstrom of swirling boats and debris.

Cuthbert waited for the next onslaught. It came 55 minutes later, with less force but more height. Again, the heavy scow was whirled around and around and battered its way through buildings and came to rest upright on a crushed store.

The third wave, less violent still, refloated the scow and Cuthbert tied a line to a telephone pole. Through the night, just about every 55 minutes, the waves came in weaker each time until the nightmare ended at 3 a.m.

Trooper Church, still at his radio, was trying to contact each of the tiny, remote villages on the island. In days to come, he would visit each personally. Some show on maps, others only in the trooper's notebook. How are the Munsens? Church would fly out to see. The Martins? All five of them were missing, no trace of their cattle ranch. Village by village, family by family, he would count them all.

But on this Good Friday night there were two villages he could not reach by radio: Afognak and Ouzinkie. He dispatched fishing boats to both places. Then he began contacting fishing boats. Most replied. Others didn't, ominously. The *Selief* did.

"*Selief, Selief,* where are you?"

"It looks," answered Cuthbert, "as though I'm in the back of the Kodiak schoolhouse, five blocks from the shoreline."

Because of Church's radio warnings, most of the people in the villages escaped. A few are still missing. But in at least four cases—Afognak, Ouzinkie, Kaguyak and Old Harbor—the destruction was almost complete. Only a handful of houses remained. Timbers of others slapped at the shore and other houses, still intact, were driven miles across the water to distant beaches.

And now suddenly it was over.

The sea became serene again. The roar of the wall of water and tumbling houses and boats was gone.

Throughout the broad earthquake area, Alaskans began picking up the debris in search of bodies. By week's end, the total of known dead and presumed dead was 125. ▨

32

Urban Renewal on the Last Frontier, 1964-1969

by *Morgan Sherwood*

The availability of federal reconstruction funds lured policy makers to opt for urban renewal rather than rehabilitation. The result was an economic, social and aesthetic disaster.

Alaskans began to recuperate soon after the paroxysm ended, thanks in part to the ingestion of a large dose of federal relief and rehabilitation money. The earthquake affected different regions in the Cook Inlet area differently, and the reaction of each community varied. Although Seldovia escaped with relatively little damage, a general subsidence of the shoreline confronted citizens of the old town with a difficult choice. How the choice was made and what happened thereafter, to 1970, is described in the following document; the article should be considered an example of contemporary reporting rather than definitive history.

*I*n the last decade, the new environmental crusaders in and out of Alaska have come to fear the combined power of large out-of-state extractive industries and an in-state faction comprised of some town businessmen and lawyers steeped in the frontier exploitive ethic. Non-selective, slash timber cutting in Southeastern Alaska's national forest, oilwell platforms in Cook Inlet, oil tanker traffic along the coasts, and an oil pipeline stretching from the Arctic to the Gulf of Alaska, all seem to threaten to erase once and for all America's "last frontier." The economic ramifications are equally alarming to those residents who came to Alaska precisely because of its beauty and sparse population. One of those ramifications is the threat posed by the new extractive corporations to the country's old, renewable resource industries, fishing and tourism. Polluted bays, eroded streams, and cut-over landscapes do not attract salmon or tourists.

The political match should not however be described simply as a contest between frontier entrepreneurs on the make and oil-lumber firms on the one side, and established industries and conservationists inside and outside of the state. A fifth power in most decisions of how Alaska will go in the future is the federal government. Its role historically has been to preserve the territory's natural resources, but since Alaska achieved statehood in 1958, the central government's behavior on environmental questions has often been contradictory. The Department of Agriculture permits private lumber companies to scrape bald the mountains along the lovely fiords of Alaska's famed "Inside Passage." The Interior Department delayed construction of the trans-Alaskan petroleum pipeline, and then sanctioned it. And the Justice Department is now pursuing a legal suit to give away to the world much of Cook Inlet, a body of water which, like Chesapeake Bay, has been historically under the jurisdiction of the country whose flag flew on shore; such a change in the legal status of Cook Inlet would make efficient conservation administration extremely difficult if not impossible. The federal government's behavior in the matter of Seldovia is yet another example of Washington's ambiguous Alaskan policy. The town was almost urban-renewed out of existence.

Seldovia takes its name (a variation of the Russian word for herring) from the nearby bay. Though its early history is dim, the town probably existed before Russia sold Alaska to the United States in 1867. Seldovia profited from the influx of gold seekers around the turn of the century, and not too long thereafter settled down to a picturesque existence as the largest fishing village on the southern shores of Cook Inlet. There are no roads or railroads into Seldovia. Marine transportation and a small airstrip tie it to other parts of Alaska.

The town is located near the southwestern end of Kachemak Bay, an easterly arm of the Inlet. The southern littoral of Kachemak Bay is blessed with marine alpine scenery: Steep and rugged mountains, cut by impressive glaciers, smaller bays and fiords, and bordered by a sinuous coast dotted offshore by thickly forested islands. In comparison to similar landscapes in Southeastern Alaska or on Prince William Sound, the weather on Kachemak is relatively mild and dry.

The old fishing village of Seldovia fitted comfortably in these impressive surroundings. The business section and a goodly part of the residential district were built along a boardwalk ten feet wide, set on pilings stabbed into the beach and abutting the bluff. No visitor was likely to forget his first views of Seldovia: the boat harbor, the fine old log and frame buildings clustered together on their centipedal legs, the fishing boats disgorging their catch at one of the cannery docks while other boats, tethered behind a grocery or liquor store, loaded supplies. A large freighter, looking out of place, might be cranking palettes of canned fish aboard. A leisurely shopper needed only to dodge a bicycle or two on the town's "main street," one end of which led to the Slough and its lovely little houses ashore, some with neatly tended yards; skiffs were tied along the banks of the Slough, perhaps to a greying warehouse also on stilts. Beyond the other end of the boardwalk was the old graveyard. Overlooking the town, in the Russian style, was the small Orthodox Church on the bluff.

Seldovia's charm was human as well as environmental. The town's reputation for hospitality and fun was surpassed by no other Alaskan village. Old Seldovia's Fourth of July celebration, just before the fishermen left to hunt the salmon in earnest, was famous throughout the territory for old-fashioned frontier hilarity. Seldovians even had their own verbal accent, deriving possibly from the Russian creole past and retained by relative isolation.

What happened to Seldovia was the Alaskan Earthquake of 1964, but indirectly, for there was no structural damage except a tide-wrecked small boat harbor which the Corps of Engineers rebuilt promptly. The earthquake did, however, result in a three and one-half foot subsidence of Kenai Peninsula on which Seldovia nestles (while on the eastern side of the earthquake fault, along Prince William Sound, some land rose more than 25 feet). For Seldovia, that meant the highest tides would cover the boardwalk and invade the first story of any structure built on the boardwalk, whether home, shop or cannery.

The federal government was quick to offer solace by promising funds. The State . . . was quick to accept disaster relief; Alaska was at the time of the Great Quake suffering a slump from decreased federal spending for defense. The alternatives were: (1) raise the Seldovia boardwalk and its buildings, or (2) destroy the boardwalk then dike and fill. The last is a favorite solution of the Army Corps of Engineers for almost any engineering problem.

The Corps, as agent of the Office of Emergency Planning during the initial survey, considered raising the boardwalk for about $700,000. The project might have cost $1 million, and would not have included any stores or homes. The job of rehabilitation could have been done, according to an engineer closely associated with the situation, but it was not financially feasible. By "financially feasible" the engineer meant that rehabilitation of all of the old town would have been less expensive than the $4½ million eventually spent to destroy it, but rehabilitation would not have

207

been economical in the long run. We know what Lord Keynes said about the "long run."

None of this explains satisfactorily why the city rejected rehabilitation. One State official admits the town was not kept informed during the early confusion. A "feasibility survey for urban renewal" was undertaken by an Oregon firm; most of its recommendations were never carried out. At least one of its observations was in error; the firm overestimated the cost of maintaining the 3250 foot boardwalk. One suggestion for a boulder dike directly in front of the town was apparently rejected. Still another recommendation by the Oregonians was decidedly prescient: the failure to raise or relocate buildings by the fall of 1964 would result in the loss of employment and possibly the loss of the fishing industry.

For whatever reasons, five of the six city councilmen present at a meeting in September of 1964 resolved that Seldovia's problems could not be solved by rehabilitating the old town. (In the previous month, four city councilmen had telegraphed the Alaska State Housing Authority in Anchorage, the bureau which became the instrument of federal urban renewal. The telegram stated that any limited type of urban renewal "would stagnate the future growth and development of Seldovia"; they wrote as "councilmen and representing the people of Seldovia" and wanted *total* renewal.)

After the Council's decision of late September to reject rehabilitation, the issue was more easily defined: should Seldovia permit the State Housing Authority, directing the Corps of Engineers and its contractors, to buy out all property owners on the boardwalk, destroy the old town, and replace it by gravel and rock fill? Several exciting public meetings were held over the issue. The City Council held special meetings, and the State Housing Authority sent representatives to argue for all or nothing. The fish canneries made their position clear to the townspeople, most of whom were economically dependent on the canneries: if urban renewal were not approved, the canneries would move out. The region's State legislator, a young Republican named Clem Tillion, urged rehabilitation of the old boardwalk, as did Jack English, a Democrat and Seldovia's senior civic leader. A full slate of opposition Council candidates was mustered for the upcoming City election, so six of the incumbents urged the Housing Authority to submit certain resolutions for Council consideration before the election. Then a democratic facade was erected when citizen opinion was tallied. On October 12, 1964, 136 Seldovians favored urban renewal and 54 did not. The City Council endorsed the go-ahead.

Seldovians were never given a chance to vote secretly on a referendum. The 136-54 "vote" was no more than an opinion poll, with everybody's opinion public knowledge. The Council could have acted without the opinion poll, because the law does not require secret elections on such issues even when the future welfare of each elector is affected directly, and the survival of a whole town is at stake.

The controversy was pretty heady stuff. It moved one Seldovian, Mrs. Elsa Pedersen, to incorporate the story in a children's book, *House Upon A Rock* (Atheneum, 1968). The scene Mrs. Pedersen sets in her fictionalized version was not the same situation facing Seldovia after the earthquake. "Fidalgo" was, in *House Upon A Rock*, a "desolute ruin" after the tremor, its industries and businesses destroyed. The alternatives were to rebuild completely the boardwalk of "Fidalgo" (which was "danged expensive too") or to dike and fill. Though circumstances and choices in Fidalgo and Seldovia differed, part of the argument must have been similar. In Fidalgo, the good guys opt for Progress, automobiles and all.

> "The boardwalk was put up forty years ago, and it served our purpose all that time. Let's not change for no reason at all."
>
> "Forty years ago we didn't have dozens of cars in town either," Derrick heard his father cry. "You can't keep them off the boardwalk, but it ain't suitable for traffic either." . . .
>
> "But it won't be Fidalgo," Arsentie Heintzman protested. "Whenever anyone thinks of this town, he thinks of the boardwalk. We've got to build it back."
>
> "Horsefeathers!" Willie Slocum snorted. "There's more to Fidalgo than the boardwalk. Why not grab this chance to be a modern town? It's our salvation, if we want to progress."

In a hairy Fidalgo "election," the citizens vote against pilings and for gravel, the future, and the younger generation, one of whom reminds them: "'There's the oil industry, too,' he cried, 'Don't forget that. My dad says it's going to be the biggest field in North America, right here in Cook Inlet.'"

With the Council's nod, the Housing Authority began to purchase property along Seldovia's shoreline. Some cannery spokesmen, say angry citizens, had come dangerously close to intimidation by threatening to leave Seldovia if urban renewal were rejected. Urban renewal was not rejected, and the canneries left. The price paid to seafood processing plants by the ASHA was (to borrow a phrase from an unpublished Council study made in 1968) "get-away" money. If the government had provided rehabilitation funds, the plants might have stayed a few years to protect their overall investment. Instead, . . . [the] purchases by urban renewal were irresistible. The fishing industry on Cook Inlet was in a "rationalization" phase; that is, mergers and closures were underway to make the industry more efficient and profitable. Seldovia's decision unhappily coincided with a reshuffling of the Cook Inlet-Kodiak industry. One king crab plant, which had promised to return, did in fact construct a new installation in town. . . . [But] the retention of one basic industry was not, by 1968, the salvation of Seldovia. Its City Council in that year pleaded for the deferral of payment on certain bonds, citing the loss of income: before urban renewal there were five seafood processors with a labor force of 200, and now there is one employing 60.

Blasting, bulldozing and gravel-filling began in earnest in 1965 and was still underway in 1966. The project manager (formerly a City Councilman strongly in favor of urban renewal), estimated that thirty-five families and twenty-four businesses were being displaced. Some 250 old Russian graves were replanted elsewhere to resemble a miniature Flanders Field. The cost to the American taxpayer of the disinterment was $140,879.

Jack English requested a zoning variance for his home, which according to plans would be in a "marine-oriented commercial" area. More than one councilman sympathized with English, who came to town in 1923 and whose wife had resided there even longer. One councilman did not like the idea. He said the project should "go for the future" and that Seldovia could not "sacrifice industry for one person." . . . Eventually, a "declaration of taking" was executed. English was asked by an ASHA representative for rent on the home to which English had had clear title for several years.

Former Mayor Richard Inglima wrote to the project office in early 1966, wondering where he, his family and business could relocate temporarily. His family—six adults and one child living in a five-bedroom home—were being asked to stay in a small three-bedroom trailer, despite an urban renewal plan submitted to the City and stating that "temporary relocation will be no less desirable in character than the dwelling being vacated." Inglima had been told to operate his store and warehouse from the basement of his home. He noted poignantly how the problem had been eased somewhat, since twenty families and nine businesses departed Seldovia after they were bought out by the Housing Authority.

Old Seldovia soon lay buried under the new Alaska's dream of Progress. Four of its five basic industries are gone. The boardwalk has disappeared and only a part of the Slough district hints at the charm of the old town. A gray plateau of gravel that now comprises downtown Seldovia is spotted with a handful of ugly, prefabricated metal buildings. A few autos dart back and forth and nowhere, leaving clouds of dust in their tracks. A great gash marks the cut made in the bluff below the Russian Church, and the Church's facade is partially obfuscated by, among other things, a couple of house trailers. Estimates place the population at one-half of the pre-renewal figure. Few people walk the main street and the new small boat harbor is almost empty. The school population in 1969 was down from 120 to 60; one-half of the younger generation to whom Elsa Pedersen dedicated a resurrected "Fidalgo," have left—and so has Elsa Pedersen. Half the independent fishermen operating out of Seldovia have taken up residence in other places. Fishermen living in isolated locales on the Peninsula now deliver their fish elsewhere and shop elsewhere too. Many of the post-school, younger Seldovians resent bitterly the fate of their town, as do numerous older Alaskans who knew and loved the frontier city.

Seldovia may rise again. For many reasons, it deserves another chance, though it's difficult to avoid the conclusion that Seldovia, like Little Rollo, "brought it on himself." The harbor still remains. The physical setting is still there, although the town no longer complements its topographical surroundings. One of the minor mishappenstances in the story was that as Seldovia tore down its major tourist attractions, the State was beginning tourist ferryboat service from Kodiak to Homer via Seldovia. The City Council still has hope for tourism and may get a few sightseers if the city rebuilds intelligently. The main hope of the town, however, is in logging.

A timber firm is slash-cutting trees nearby, some of them in the watercourses of salmon spawning streams, and carting the timber overland to the previously unsoiled south shore of Kachemak Bay, where a mill squares the logs before a Japanese ship loads the wood for transport to Asia. At present, eight families engaged in the industry live in Seldovia and are flown to the mill. A twenty-mile road between Seldovia and the mill site is under construction. The lumber business will eventually employ twenty men for ten years. The *Anchorage Times* reported: "New growth could be suitable for pulp wood harvesting within 80 years," according to the Oregon logger, Mr. Christian. The town, having destroyed itself with the help of the state and federal governments, now pins its immediate future on the destruction of the surrounding countryside.

Seldovia's melancholy experience is more than a showcase for misdirected ambitions and policies. It illustrates another of Alaska's dilemmas. To apply unmodified in the new state current answers to the problems of urban America, can be cruel and wasteful. Continued acceptance of the old frontier exploitive ethic will be equally ruinous. The question is: How to avoid these ugly and extreme alternatives?

33

Who Owns
Cook Inlet? (1974)

by Judges Koelsch,
Carter & Wallace

*The essence of the controversy involved the proper
location of the Alaska coastline.*

*I*nformation in the preceding documents should lead almost
anyone to the conclusion that Cook Inlet "belonged" to the people
who lived along its shores, and that Cook Inlet begins at the Barren
Islands, with Cape Douglas on the west and Cape Elizabeth or Gore
Point on the east, not that the Inlet begins just south of Kalgin Island.
But lawyers will be lawyers. Recently federal attorneys were asked by
their political superiors to prevent the State of Alaska from leasing
undersea resources south of Kalgin, claiming the southern Inlet was
international, or at most territorial. The State lawyers insisted that
Cook Inlet was a "closed sea," or "historic bay" like Chesapeake, and

had always been considered an inland waterway. On the face of it, the major issue was the sordid question of who would profit from underwater petroleum. The implications were larger, however, and involved an apparent attempt by the national government to give away a chunk of Alaska; Alaska is a maritime province and its related rights, during the last few decades, have occasionally been bargained away by Washington in exchange for some doubtful diplomatic advantage abroad. A federal victory might also have led to jurisdictional disputes over resource conservation policy, between the State, the national government and foreign countries, and not just over mineral resources but over the fisheries and other biologic resources as well. Finally, the controversy is another example of how questions of historic truth are frequently left to lawyers. Happily, in this case, the victorious attorneys were on the side of history, though not because the record was clear but because it was not "clearly erroneous."

The following opinion of the San Francisco U.S. Court of Appeals was delivered in March 1974. It concludes our anthology of Cook Inlet historical curiosities with a variant of the same question of territoriality addressed implicitly and explicitly early in the collection.

*T*he United States sued the State of Alaska to quiet title to
the lower part of Cook Inlet located on the Alaska coast
and to enjoin Alaska from offering oil and gas leases for sale in the
area. The district court found in favor of Alaska [1972]. The United
States appealed and we affirm.

In early 1967, Alaska offered to sell, at competitive bidding, an
oil and gas lease to a tract of 2,500 acres of submerged lands
located in lower Cook Inlet. The United States does not contest
Alaska's right to the upper part of Cook Inlet. The tract in
question, however, is located more than 3 geographic miles
seaward of the low-water line, the closing lines of rivers and small
bays within Cook Inlet and the 24-mile fallback line drawn across
the narrows at Kalgin Island. The essence of the controversy
involves the proper location of the Alaska coastline. The United
States would place the coastline at the 24-mile fallback line at
Kalgin Island. Alaska would place it at the 47-mile opening of
Cook Inlet extending from Cape Douglas through the Barren
Islands to Point Gore. The significance of the placement of this line
is that under the Submerged Lands Act of 1953, a state is entitled
to the natural resources of the seabed and subsoil in waters up to
3 geographic miles seaward from the state's coast line at low tide or
its functional equivalent as drawn by connecting the land openings
of water inlets such as rivers and small bays. The waters landward
from the line forming the functional equivalent of the coast line are

215

inland waters belonging to the state and the 3-mile distance extends seaward from that line. Whether this line should be drawn at Kalgin Island (as the United States contends) or at Cape Douglas-Point Gore (as Alaska contends) will determine whether the area in question may be leased by Alaska. The pivotal question in this determination is whether this is a seabed over which there are "inland waters" as denominated in, but not defined by, the Submerged Lands Act. If so, Alaska is correct and the district court's judgment must be affirmed.

The Supreme Court has adopted the definition of inland waters as contained in the Convention on the Territorial Sea and the Contiguous Zone. Article 7 describes inland bays; but Cook Inlet fails to meet the definition which requires a distance of no more than 24 miles between the natural entrance points of the bay. Cook Inlet is 47 miles wide at its natural entrance points. Nevertheless, the Court has recognized that whether or not a body of water is inland may depend upon historical as well as geographical factors. The Court has stated:

> Certain shoreline configurations have been deemed to confine bodies of water, such as bays, which are necessarily inland. But it has also been recognized that other areas of water closely connected to the shore, although they do not meet any precise geographical test, may have achieved the status of inland waters by the manner in which they have been treated by the coastal nation.

Historic bays, which Article 7 exempts from the requirement of being no more than 24 miles between the natural entrance points, fall within this classification. As to such waters the Court in the *Louisiana Boundary Case* [1969] continued: "[I]t is generally agreed that historic title can be claimed only when the 'coastal nation has traditionally asserted and maintained dominion with the acquiescence of foreign nations.'" As further guidance the Court noted with apparent approval:

> A recent United Nations study recommended by the International Law Commission reached the following conclusions [for "State" read "nation"]:
> "There seems to be fairly general agreement that at least three factors have to be taken into consideration in determining whether a State has acquired a historic title to a maritime area.

These factors are : (1) the exercise of authority over the area by the State claiming the historic right; (2) the continuity of this exercise of authority; (3) the attitude of foreign States. First, the State must exercise authority over the area in question in order to acquire a historic title to it. Secondly, such exercise of authority must have continued for a considerable time; indeed it must have developed into a usage. More controversial is the third factor, the position which the foreign States may have taken towards this exercise of authority. Some writers assert that the acquiescence of other States is required for the emergence of an historic title; others think that absence of opposition by these States is sufficient."

The district court correctly adopted and applied this three-pronged test. Having correctly applied the law, our sole remaining task is to determine whether the facts found by the trial court were clearly erroneous.

The United States mounts a heavy attack, reviewing in detail evidence which it contends leads unquestionably to the conclusion that the waters involved are at the most territorial rather than inland. It has succeeded in demonstrating that the evidence was in conflict and that the question of determining the ultimate inferences to be drawn was close. But it failed to show the findings to be clearly erroneous. The trial judge received the testimony of hundreds of witnesses and examined volumes of documents. . . .

* * *

As the law applied by the district court was correct and its findings were not clearly erroneous, we affirm.

Notes

(by document number)

1. de Laguna, *The Archaeology of Cook Inlet* (Philadelphia: University of Pennsylvania, 1934) 148-154; used with permission. For a recent summary of the scholarship, see Hans-Georg Bandi, *Eskimo Prehistory*, translated by A. E. Keep (College: University of Alaska, 1969). The Chirikov quotation is from F. A. Golder, editor, *Bering's Voyages* (New York: Octagon, 1968; 2 vols.) I, 298.

2. *Ethnography of the Tanaina* (New Haven: Yale University, 1937; Publications in Anthropology #16) 28, 29, 31, 40, 41, 111-113; reprinted in 1966 by Human Relations Area Files Press, New Haven; used with permission.

3. Pierce, "An Editorial Note," in Fedorova, *The Russian Population in Alaska and California, Late 18th Century - 1867,* translated and edited by R. A. Pierce and A. S. Donnelly (Kingston, Ontario: Limestone Press, 1973; originally published in Moscow: Nauka, 1971) 316-319; used with permission.

4. *Ecological Effects of Forest Fires in the Interior of Alaska* (Washington: GPO, July 1955; U.S. Department of Agriculture Technical Bulletin #1133) 82-86.

5. (London: Strahan, Nicol and Cadell, 1784; 3 vols.) III, 385, 386, 391-398. The best edition for serious students is J. C. Beaglehole, editor, *The Journals of Captain Cook: The Voyage of the* Resolution *and* Discovery, *1776-1780* (Cambridge: Cambridge University for the Hakluyt Society, 1967) III, Part 1, 359 passim.

6. George Dixon, editor, *A Voyage Round the World . . . 1785, 1786, 1787, 1788 . . .* (London: Goulding, 1789) 58-68. Portlock's book is more informative and not as fussy as Beresford's letters: *Voyage Round the World . . . 1785, 1786, 1787 and 1788* (London: Stockdale and Goulding, 1789). The French expedition to which Beresford refers was probably that of the Comte de La Perouse, who did not reach Cook Inlet.

7. From A. I. Andreyev, editor, *Russian Discoveries in the Pacific and in North America in the Eighteenth and Nineteenth Centuries*, translated by C. Ginsburg (Ann Arbor, Michigan: J. W. Edwards for the American Council of Learned Societies) 104-107; used with permission. The Spanish ships were probably the *Princesa* commanded by Estéban José Martinez, and the *San Carlos* under Gonzalo Lopez de Haro.

8. From P. A. Tikhmenev, *Historical Review of the Formation of the Russian-American Company and Its Activity to the Present Time* (St. Petersburg: in Russian, 1861-63; 2 vols.) I, 41 ff; manuscript translation by R. A. Pierce, used with his permission. See also, Document #15.

9. *A Voyage of Discovery to the North Pacific Ocean and Round the World . . . Performed in the Years 1790, 1791, 1792, 1793, 1794, and 1795, in the* Discovery *Sloop of War, and Armed Tender* Chatham (London: Robinson and Edwards, 1798; 3 vols.) III, 140-143; paragraphing added. For more about Vancouver, see Bern Anderson, *Surveyor of the Sea* (Seattle: University of Washington, 1960).

10. *History of Alaska* (San Francisco: A. L. Bancroft, 1886) 368-374. For more about Petroff, see Documents #14 and #18, and note #14.

11. "Einige Beobachtungen und Bermerkungen uber das Goldvorkommen in den Besitzungen der Russich-Amerikanishchen Compagnie," *Archiv fur Wissenschaftliche Kunde von Russland* (Berlin), 25 (1866) 235-236; translated loosely by the editor, who placed some footnotes in the text. See also, Documents #14 and #18.

12. U. S. Congress, *Congressional Globe, Appendix,* 40th Congress, 2d session (July 1, 1868) 397, 398.

13. R. G. Athearn, editor, "An Army Officer's Trip to Alaska in 1869," *Pacific Northwest Quarterly,* 40 (January 1949) 51-53; paragraphing added; used with permission. Ferdinand Bischoff's career is sketched briefly in M. Sherwood, *Exploration of Alaska, 1865-1900* (New Haven: Yale University, 1965) 23, 24.

14. "Gold Seeking in the Regions of Perpetual Snow," *San Francisco Sunday Chronicle* (December 26, 1875) 5; paragraphing and minor stylistic alterations added. There is little doubt that "Polaris" was Ivan Petroff—Bancroft's helper, director for Alaska of the Tenth U.S. Census, and a compiler of the Census of 1890; see also, Documents #10 and #18. Petroff joined the Army in Washington Territory during the summer of 1867; his desertion saved him from the discomfort of a shipwrecked *Torrent* (see Document #13). The commander of Battery "F" asked for his presence at Kenai, as a translator, and he was discharged there in July 1870. Whether he was in fact a trader or still only an army private during this journey, is moot; however (from internal evidence) he probably did make the trip, though some of the episodes along the way may be pure invention. The latest research into his whole career is R. A. Pierce, "New Light on Ivan Petroff, Historian of Alaska," *Pacific Northwest Quarterly,* 59 (January 1968) 1-10. Petroff's work on the census is summarized in P. D. Carlson, "Alaska's First Census: 1880," *The Alaska Journal,* 1 (winter 1971) 48-53.

15. A. Woldt, editor, *Capitain Jacobsen's Reise an der Nordwestkiiste Amerikas, 1881-1883* (Leipzig: Max Spohr, 1884) 360, 361, 369-371; translated loosely by the editor of this anthology.

16. Davidson, "Notes on the Volcanic Eruption of Mount St. Augustin, Alaska, October 6, 1883," *Science,* 3 (February 15, 1884) 186-189. Anonymous [Dall], "Note," ibid., 3 (June 27, 1884) 798. Compare Dall's description of the same event, in *The Nation,* 61 (September 12, 1895) 183: "A few years ago this island possessed

an excellent harbor for small craft and was the resort of native hunters. A violent eruption closed the entrance to the harbor, which is now a placid lagoon dotted with enormous volcanic blocks, ashes were carried by the wind for more than one hundred miles, the fish in the sea were cooked alive, and the inhabitants of the whole inlet were terror-stricken by tidal waves."

17. *Summer and Fall in Western Alaska* (London: H. Cox, 1903) 33-36. The Moser quotations and information are from "The Salmon and Salmon Fisheries of Alaska: Cook Inlet District," in *Report of the Operations of the United States Fish Commission Steamer* Albatross, *for the Year Ending June 30, 1898* (Washington: GPO, 1899; Bulletin of the U.S. Fish Commission, vol. 18, for 1898) 140-143. For more about salmon: R. A. Cooley, *Politics of Conservation: The Decline of the Alaska Salmon* (New York: Harper & Row, 1963).

18. *Report on the Population and Resources of Alaska at the Eleventh Census: 1890* (Washington: GPO, 1893) 72, 73; some of the spelling is up-dated without ellipses and brackets.

19. "Report on Coal and Lignite of Alaska," *Seventeenth Annual Report of the U.S. Geological Survey, 1895-96, Part 1* (Washington: GPO, 1897) 785, 786, 791-795. For more about coal mining, see R. W. Stone, "Coal Fields of the Kachemak Bay Regions," in F. H. Moffitt and R. W. Stone, *Mineral Resources of the Kenai Peninsula, Alaska* (Washington: GPO, 1906; U.S. Geological Survey Bulletin #277). For more about Dall's remarkable career, see M. Sherwood, *Exploration of Alaska* (New Haven: Yale University, 1965) chapters 2 and 3.

20. "A Reconnaissance from Resurrection Bay to the Tanana River, Alaska, 1898," *Twentieth Annual Report of the U.S. Geological Survey, 1898-99, Part 7* (Washington: GPO, 1899) 318-321, 339. A new chronicle of mining in the region is M. J. Barry, *History of Mining on the Kenai Peninsula* (Anchorage: Alaska Northwest Publishing Company, 1973).

21. *The Iniskin-Chinitna Peninsula and the Snug Harbor District, Alaska* (Washington: GPO, 1927; U.S. Geological Survey Bulletin #789) 1, 2, 49, 50.

22. "Agricultural Experiments in Alaska," *Yearbook of the Department of Agriculture, 1898* (Washington: GPO, 1899) 519-522.

23. *Natural History of the Queen Charlotte Islands, British Columbia; Natural History of the Cook Inlet Region, Alaska* (Washington: GPO, September 1901; Biological Survey North American Fauna #21) 60, 61, 53, 54. Christine Heller's *Wild Flowers of Alaska* (Portland, Oregon: Graphic Arts Center, 1966), is a beautiful guidebook that can be used easily by anyone.

24. *Summer and Fall in Western Alaska* (London: H. Cox, 1903) 47, 48, 166-171.

25. From Burroughs, "Narrative of the Expedition," *Harriman Alaska Series* (Washington: Smithsonian Institution, 1910) I, 76, 84.

26. Cook, "The Conquest of Mount McKinley," *Harper's Monthly Magazine*, 114 (May 1907) 821, 822. Browne, *The Conquest of Mt. McKinley* (New York: Putnam, 1913) 69-72. An entertaining account of Cook and the mountain is in Terris Moore, *Mt. McKinley: The Pioneer Climbs* (College: University of Alaska, 1967). Cook and

the North Pole are discussed by J. E. Weems, *Race for the Pole* (New York: Henry Holt, 1960).

27. "The Government Railroad of Alaska," *Mining and Scientific Press* 115 (December 29, 1917) 925-932. The town's earliest days are studied in W. H. Wilson, "The Founding of Anchorage: Federal Townbuilding on the Last Frontier," *Pacific Northwest Quarterly* 58 (July 1967) 130-141. For a study of the entire railway, see E. M. Fitch, *The Alaska Railroad* (New York: Praeger, 1967).

28. "Problems Confronting Early Settlers in the Matanuska Valley," in C. C. Georgeson, *Information for Prospective Settlers of Alaska* (Washington: GPO, 1917; Alaska Agricultural Experiment Station Circular #1-revised) 26-30. Early attempts by the Railroad to promote agriculture are discussed in W. H. Wilson, "The Alaskan Engineering Commission and a New Agricultural Frontier," *Agricultural History*, 42 (October 1968) 339-350.

29. "A Petroleum Seepage near Anchorage," in Brooks and others, *Mineral Resources of Alaska - 1921* (Washington: GPO, 1923; U.S. Geological Survey Bulletin #739) 133-135.

30. *Present and Potential Agricultural Areas in Alaska* (Palmer: University of Alaska, Alaska Agricultural Experiment Station, Bulletin #15, February 1953) 9-12. The figures for 1964 were determined in the following way: from the *Congressional Record*, 89th Congress, 2d session (November 10, 1966) Appendix, pp. A5684-A5686, all expenditures of the U.S.D.A. in Alaska for 1959-1966 (except for the Forest Service and $30 million in R.E.A. special earthquake funds), were divided by eight, for the average annual expenditure; figures for the annual product value and for the number of farms were taken from D. N. Jones, "Alaska's Economy," *Alaska Review*, 2 (fall, winter, 1966-67) 6, 20. A social history of the Matanuska colony is E. Atwood, *We Shall Be Remembered* (Anchorage: Alaska Methodist University, 1966).

31. "A Wild Maelstrom of Boats," *Anchorage Daily Times* (April 14, 1964) 62, 63; used with permission.

32. "Urban Renewal on the Last Frontier: A Point of View," *International Journal of Environmental Studies* (England), 1 (March 1971) 211-217; used with permission. The lead quotation is from the abstract of the paper, appearing on p. 211.

33. U.S. Court of Appeals for the Ninth District (San Francisco), "Opinion, *U.S.A. vs. State of Alaska*," No. 73-2400 (March 19, 1974) 1-4.

The Cook Inlet Area

Scale in Miles

0   50   100   200

CartoGraphics by Jon.Hersh, Alaska Northwest Publishing Company

ALASKA

Map Location →

Aleutian Islands

Shumagin
Islands

Ilian

Iliamr
Lake

Bristol Bay

ALASKA PENINSULA

9835

The Cook Inlet collection: two hundred years of
      selected Alaskan history, edited by Morgan
      Sherwood; illus. by Diana Tillion.   Anchorage,
      Alaska Northwest Pub. Co., c1974.
      xii, 222p., ₍2₎ leaves of plates, map.   22cm.

      Includes bibliographical references.

1.Cook Inlet region, Alaska-History-Miscellanea.
2.Alaska-History.   I.Sherwood, Morgan B.